BORN TO FLY

Also by Margaret Silf:

At Sea with God
Daily Readings with Margaret Silf
Faith
Hidden Wings
Landmarks
Roots and Wings
Taste and See
The Miller's Tale and Other Parables
The Other Side of Chaos
Wayfaring

All published by Darton, Longman and Todd

BORN TO FLY

A HANDBOOK FOR BUTTERFLIES-IN-WAITING

MARGARET SILF

DARTON · LONGMAN + TODD

Pour les enfants du monde: l'avenir vous appartient

Für die Kinder der Welt: Euch gehört die Zukunft

For the children of the world: the future is yours

First published in Great Britain in 2017 by
Darton, Longman and Todd Ltd
1 Spencer Court
140–142 Wandsworth High Street
London SW18 4JJ

ISBN 978-0-232-53331-6

A catalogue record for this book is available from the British Library.

Designed and produced by Judy Linard
Printed and bound by Bell and Bain, Glasgow

CONTENTS

ALPHA

When Ron and Ali moved into the cul-de-sac a fresh breeze stirred through the neighbourhood, rippling our piles of rotting leaves and winter-dead debris like a spring storm come too early, the January kicking of a child not expected until March. Unsettling a set-in-its-ways solidity. Dissolving it into rustles of mirth.

The first conversation, conducted in their driveway with practised civility and all the conventional expressions of well-coming and well-wishing, revealed instantly that this would be a soul-friendship. Ali's spirit spilled over our fences. It was never going to be something you could ignore, or would ever again want to be without.

The second conversation was on our doorstep. Eyes downcast she stood there, abject in her mortification, not knowing how to tell us that she had reversed her car into our garden wall. And even in her apologising, she somehow kept bubbling. It was hard to be cross. We followed her, to view the damage. Just a few stones dislodged. We stood there alongside her, all of us outright laughing at the ridiculous sight of our borders breached, our downed defences. The friendship was sealed in that moment.

Spring passed too soon. An irritating pimple. A tiny swelling. Could be something to worry about. She didn't know. Forty-something, full of life, and a little rising of the skin to threaten everything. She didn't do religion. Never exposed to the story of her original sin and need for official cleansing. But something had seeped inside, in spite of all, leading her to ask what she could have done so wrong to deserve this. A little spiteful snake, telling her *the Great Lie, denying the life that ran through her like a stream, obscuring joy with guilt unfounded.*

Shadows fell. Yet one bright candle glowed. The sense of an ending, but, she declared, she would return as a black butterfly and we would know all was well. We smiled. Typical of Ali we thought mischievously.

Middle of the night. Short staffed and an emergency on another ward. A seizure, temporarily unattended. Ali was gone. A light went out in the cul-de-sac.

At the funeral the church was packed, but Ron was gone too deep into the well of his loneliness to notice. Only the slow-rising tide of tears would raise him eventually to life-light again. But everyone else that day noticed the arrival, through some unstopped crack in the church door, of the mysterious mourner – black, but winged. Alighting now and again on some bowed head or shaking shoulder, as if to say: I told you so.

Afterwards the wake was full of the story. Did you see her? She landed on my shoulder. She always said she would. Typical Ali to pull a stunt like that. Only Ron hadn't seen. Maybe he didn't need to see. Maybe he had a different kind of seeing, down in his dark.

It was never quite a cul-de-sac after that. A few stones dislodged made it into a thoroughfare. A way through the dark. The naked invisible armour of trust that protects through the valley. The compass of joy that points to something more, now winged and indestructible.

The dream that outlives all the dreamers.
Outlives and fulfils them.
The Alpha that points towards the Omega.

Ali's story drifts across the morning air as we begin our adventure into the miracle of flight still curled up inside us, dormant. Ordinary caterpillar beginnings – a good life, attentive to the needs of others even as she was attentive to her own pursuit of happiness and love. But in every *ordinary* lies the added personal ingredient turning it into *extra-ordinary*. In Ali the *extra* was impossible to overlook. It brimmed out of her and flooded the space around her, energising all of us with her vibrant presence, somehow bringing all of us into resonance with the music of who she was, just as the imaginal cells in the caterpillar resonate on their own frequency, and gradually learn to resonate with each other.

And then the cliff edge. The crisis carrying mortal danger, that would become her flight instructor. I think she would have loved the idea of the imaginal cell, because she always knew her inner butterfly, even – especially – when she was in the terrible dissolution of the chrysalis of her illness. She knew her butterfly with all the conviction of one who can say: I will not merely die, but *fly*. With Ali, you could already see the colours of her butterfly showing through the transparency of her chrysalis.

Ali was born to fly, no less than you and I. The purpose of this book is to discover ways to engage with this adventure in our real lives. You will gain most from using this book if you are familiar with its companion *Hidden Wings*, which recounts the story of transformation so familiar to us from the journey of the caterpillar through the chrysalis to the butterfly. The story is told from the point of view of the imaginal cell – one of the cells that, right from the moment the egg is laid, carries within itself the embryonic reality of the future mature butterfly – the *imago*.

Now we take that story further by applying its wisdom to our own lives, asking: can our caterpillar existence as human beings on planet Earth really be transformed into something wholly new and yet already present deep within us? How can we co-operate in practice with this dynamic of transformation and metamorphosis?

Born to Fly has two parts. Part 1 provides some necessary pre-flight instruction. Or, to change the metaphor, it serves as something of an ante-natal class to help us more effectively birth the new creation we are invited to become. It does this by posing some important questions:

- Is humanity going anywhere or is this the end of the line?

- What kind of future do we desire for ourselves, for those who follow after us, and for the whole of creation?

- Will the future simply arrive, forcing itself upon us, or can we shape that future by our own choices?

- Are we engaged in a process of spiritual, as well as physical, evolution, and if so how might we understand this better, and learn to embrace it pro-actively?

- If our choices are shaping our future, how might we learn to make those choices more wisely?

In Part 2 we take a gentle journey in five stages through the process of transformation mapped out for us by the caterpillar as it changes from a pesky garden grub, *taking* what it wants without regard for the rest of creation, to a 'flying flower', *giving* life wherever it lands.

You might choose to explore the journey in the companionship of other fellow travellers. If so, be mindful of the ancient indigenous wisdom applied in such gatherings:

- Allow each person to speak if they so wish, without interruption or any attempt to argue or correct. Some indigenous peoples use a *talking stick* to be held by the person speaking, and then passed on to the next person who wishes to share a reflection or an insight. It doesn't have to be a stick! But some token of respect for the person speaking can be helpful, reminding others to observe a listening silence.

- Don't dominate the group or permit others to do so. Ensure that each person has a fair amount of time to share what they wish to share.

- Gather on neutral ground, preferably in each other's homes, maybe rotating the hospitality, but don't overdo the hospitality or let it become competitive.

- Above all, *listen*. Listening doesn't mean waiting until the person speaking has finished so that you can start. It means listening with the heart, because you may just hear something that will change or modify some part of that heart, and in this way change the direction of the future. Listening means assuming that the other person has something important to bring to the gathering, quite possibly something more important than our own offerings.

- When each person has had an opportunity to speak, it may be helpful to open up the conversation more generally and share the responses of the gathered group.

However you choose to use this material, take the time to reflect deeply on the issues raised. This is your future that is being shaped, and the future of your grandchildren, and all who follow us in generations still to come. Quaker wisdom would urge you to hold these matters, and all whom they concern 'in the light'. Other traditions speak of prayer or meditation. It doesn't matter what we call it, but it needs to be at the heart of all our deliberations about the future of humanity on planet Earth because everything we think we are is held in a mystery infinitely greater than ourselves and guided by a sacred spirit infinitely wiser than our own.

This is our Alpha, our setting off point towards the fullness of everything we can be – towards the Omega.

SOME MAPS
FOR THE
JOURNEY

A KEY TO THE KINGDOM?

Three-year-old Isabella is writing a letter to Santa. Her mum is encouraging her to think about what she might like to receive from Santa's bounty, and is bemused to hear that the only item on the wish-list is – a key.

'A key?' she enquires. 'What kind of a key?'

The child hesitates. Mum, intrigued, continues to pursue the matter:

'Keys are usually for unlocking things. What is it you want to unlock with your key?' she asks.

No hesitation now. The confident reply comes instantly: 'A car like Mummy's.'

This incident takes its place, of course, in the family annals – probably to make another appearance at her coming-of-age party. But it makes me think of the great work upon which we are about to embark.

The secret we are hoping to unlock is the future of humanity (even more ambitious than Isabella's aspirations). Not by gazing into a crystal ball or consulting an oracle. Not by ordering what we want from some heavenly website. But by making personal and collective choices that move humanity a little closer to the fullness of all we could be.

And the key, for our purposes, is *the imaginal cell*. In the Christian tradition the fullness of life in its best possible version is commonly called the Kingdom of Heaven. Different religious traditions have their own interpretations of what this 'fullness of life', or 'heaven' is: (for example, *Shamayim* in Judaism, *Jannah* in Islam) or the concept of the highest possible plane of being (*Moksha* in Hinduism, *Nirvana* in Buddhism). This 'best version of ourselves' is clearly seen as a state of being towards which we can strive on earth, through the choices we make and the ways in which we live and relate to each other and to all creation. By living in this intentional way we too ascend, as it were, to higher levels of consciousness, more and more closely aligned with the depth of the holy mystery in whom we live and move and have our being, however we understand or imagine that mystery.

Why is the imaginal cell the key to such heights? Well of course it is a metaphor, but a very apt one, from the heart of the very real metamorphosis of the caterpillar into the butterfly. If you are familiar with this book's precursor, *Hidden Wings*, you will appreciate the pivotal role played by the (very real and not at all imaginary) imaginal cell in this amazing process.

So before we move on, let's just remind ourselves: some cells within the caterpillar, although sharing the same DNA, differ from the majority of the cells in significant ways. Biologists report that they 'resonate on a different frequency' from the others, and that they hold the blueprint for what will become the various parts of the future butterfly. These are the *imaginal cells*, so called because they hold the embryonic components of the *imago*, the mature insect.

Initially the imaginal cells operate independently as single-cell organisms, but the caterpillar's immune system regards them as a threat, attacks them, drenching them in juvenile hormone to suppress their activation during the caterpillar stage of the cycle. The imaginal cells persist, however, multiply and begin to connect with each other, forming clusters, and start to resonate at the new frequency of the emerging butterfly, sharing information among themselves. In the chrysalis stage, they reach critical mass, and begin to function as a coherent multi-cell organism as, in the fullness of time, they become the butterfly.

This is the biological story. Not surprisingly, however, the term imaginal cell has also been applied to visionary leaders who imagine a better future for life on our planet and strive, with others, to make this future a reality.

The premise of this book is that each of us is an imaginal cell, whether we have awakened to that fact or not. Ancient wisdom teaches that 'the kingdom is very near to you'; indeed that 'the kingdom is within you.' The future we long for already lies within us, awaiting its birthing time. Perhaps it has much in common with an unborn child. The coming life can weigh heavily upon a pregnant woman, demanding a great deal of her energy. The birthing itself will not be without its travails and the struggle to bring forth the future cannot be circumvented. The process will tear us apart as the new beginning emerges into our consciousness. Every parent knows that the birth of the first child changes absolutely everything. Life will never be the same again. Parturition demands of us that we let go of all that has gone before and embrace a future that has now been placed, often screaming, into our arms. The way this future grows up will be very largely shaped by us who have birthed it, whether this is a new-born child or a whole new stage of our human and spiritual evolution.

We are in travail now, throughout all our societies and nations and in our relationship with the planet itself. There's a lot of pain around and a lot of screaming happening. The birth pangs can feel excruciating – a word which in itself, for readers from the Christian tradition, immediately summons images of the cross. The imaginal cells undergo their own crucifixion in the suffocating impotence of the chrysalis. They too lie in their own tomb until time calls them into their transformed reality. The whole story speaks of life, death and resurrection, and brings that dynamic right into the heart of our own experience in the hard-pressed days of our twenty-first century, whether or not we associate ourselves with any particular spiritual tradition.

Justin Welby, Archbishop of Canterbury, described our situation like this in an address to the Church of England General Synod:

> *'We are in the middle of it all and we see neither the destination nor the road we must travel.'*

We are embarking here on a journey that attempts to reflect on what we desire that destination to be, and to make our first few tentative steps along the road we must travel.

By way of preparation we will first take a closer look at the power of the narratives that drive us, the future options before us, the dynamic of spiritual evolution in which we are engaged, and some tools to help us make our choices more wisely and intentionally as we grow gradually into the human family we can become.

THE STORIES
WE TELL
OURSELVES

Not many people could get away with writing a book about the entire history of humankind, and succeed in making it not only comprehensive but also both immensely readable and enjoyable. The story of *homo sapiens*, it transpires, is a veritable page-turner. The author of this thriller is Yuval Noah Harari. The book in question is *Sapiens: A Brief History of Humankind*.

In many ways it's a story about stories. Harari suggests – with plenty of evidence – that what distinguishes humankind from other animals is not only our superior intellect, but mainly our *imagination*. While other animals are able to communicate and to organise themselves in relatively small groups, *homo sapiens* operates on a wholly different scale. We, he says, live in two different planes of reality. On the one hand we, like all other animals, live in the observable reality of earth, hills, forests, rivers and oceans. However we also live in other realities that are not objectively 'real' but are the product of our imagination. We invent stories, and we reach surprising consensus about living by them. They determine our collective behaviour. They shape our ways of being human. Without them we would never have evolved from insignificant apes to rulers of the planet (however questionable our handling of that progression may have been).

When human beings began to weave stories to explain and

shape their lives, a whole new stage of evolution opened up. By imagining a story, it was possible to guide and influence not just the members of one's own familiar circle, but a much wider population. Harari points out that human babies are born very immature, still needing years and years of nurturing, protecting and guiding before they become independent. The stories we learn in our earliest years will shape us profoundly. Many of them will be told in good faith. But stories (or myths) can also be used to indoctrinate us, and shape our thinking and our actions in particular ways.

We could say that our stories are 'working hypotheses' to help us live and work together in large numbers. One such widespread story is the story of our nation. As children we are taught that our nation is the good guy, and we should be proud to belong to it, honour its flag, be ready to defend it with our lives if necessary. We hear, perhaps unconsciously, the mantra 'my country, right or wrong'. Then we grow up. We learn a bit of history. We are not always very proud of our own country's track record. We question whether it is always right to support our government's policies. We learn the art of dissent. We are in a different story now. We also learn, through widespread migration, that other people have a national story of their own, which has an equal right to be respected. And then we may begin to wonder whether perhaps the whole idea (or story) of a 'nation state' is going out of date as the world becomes more inter-connected, less insular. We may begin to question the wisdom of policies or choices that pull us apart from our neighbours, rather than drawing us closer together – choices that actually run counter to the direction of history itself.

Something similar happens with the religious stories we tell ourselves. We may have been taught from early years that there is a supreme being who reigns over us and will reward the good things we do and punish the bad. It's not hard to see how easily this story can be used by very mortal parents and educators to discipline and control the young, and the not-so-young. It's a bit harder to realise how much the deep-seated message of our 'sinfulness' penetrated our minds when we could have had no idea of what 'sin' might mean, or how our infant need to please those who cared for us might develop into a willingness to do almost anything to obtain divine approval as our lives moved on. Harari suggests, tongue in cheek, that 'you could never convince a monkey to give you a banana by promising him limitless bananas after death in monkey heaven' because monkeys don't do stories. Yet because of some of our religious stories we can convince millions of human beings to do something rather like that. At best our religious stories shape compassionate and respectful behaviour. But we all know how they can be distorted into shaping appalling brutality instead. Our stories are extremely important. They bestow enormous power, for either good or ill.

The thing about a story is this: if enough of us live as though the story were objectively true, then in a very real way it becomes true. Let's take the story of one who lives among us and reveals what it looks like, and what it costs, to live a human life that embodies the best, the truest and most worthy and enduring human values. To live like that has consequences. The dark side of humanity rises up in resistance and opposition, and apparently destroys such a life. But this model of the best we can be embraces the consequences, submits to the worst that the darkness can do, and ultimately transcends it, bringing new life out of apparent death. If we in turn allow this story to inspire us, and try to live by the same story ourselves, then that story takes root, grows and bears the fruits of that fullness of humanity. It *becomes* the truth it depicts. The story takes bodily form, in us. It becomes incarnate in the human story.

But stories grow and change, just as we do. According to Harari: 'Since large-scale human co-operation is based on myths, the way people co-operate can be altered by changing the myths – by telling different stories.' Sometimes this can happen very quickly. For example, during a temporary Christmas ceasefire on the Western Front in World War I, the myth changed suddenly from 'British/Germans are the enemy, so kill them' to 'We are actually all human beings and it's Christmas, so let's play football together'. The fraternisation that followed could easily have ended the hostilities, but it was rapidly reversed by the generals and the 'enemy story' was reinstated.

Stories can go out of date. We can see this very clearly in the caterpillar story. For the caterpillar the dominant story is:

- Eat all you can get

- Keep on expanding

- When you get too big, shed your outer layer and grow another one

- Defend yourself against predators, by hiding, or disguising yourself, or by deception

- If push comes to shove, get the other fellow before he gets you

- When you have had enough, or feel 'fed up', stop eating, hang upside down. You will decompose, and this is the end of the road for you.

The end of the story is a nasty mess. You won't like it, but there is nothing you can do about it. At this stage, this seems to be the whole story. The caterpillar can't know how the bigger story moves on.

For the butterfly the story goes like this:

- You will have a struggle to get free of the cocoon, but this is a birth struggle

- Take time to dry your wings in the sun. The solar energy is your fuel for the journey

- Fly above the forest and see the world from a wider perspective than anything you could have imagined when you were a caterpillar

- Choose the right kind of flower from which to take the nectar that you desire

- As you take your nectar, you will also be pollinating the flower

- You and the flower have a special relationship, each needing the other

- You will make a long journey, but you will make it in stages, like a relay race, passing on the baton of life to the next generation

- Before you die you will lay your eggs on exactly the right kind of leaf that your children will need.

Two very different stories. The caterpillar story doesn't work for the butterfly. The butterfly needs to live by a different story. We too grow out of our stories. My childhood story doesn't work for me now. But my adult story is sometimes a bigger version of the child-story – for example, I no longer believe in Santa Claus, but now I realise that the Santa story is really a story about something bigger – about the human desire to give gifts, and to do so without being recognised or thanked.

The story I learned about my country as a child also needs to grow, in recognition of the fact that I am first and foremost a global citizen, living in a particular region. My prime loyalty is to the planet and all her creatures, and not to the UK, where I happen to live.

Even more seriously, I find I have outgrown the religious story I was taught as a child, but I trust that I am growing into a bigger story based on the same deep truths and intuitions – a common ideal or 'myth' that enjoins us to love one another, and to treat each other as we would wish others to treat us – a story that draws us closer to each other and to the deep centre in whom we find our source and our destiny. This is the direction of history. It is also the direction of our souls. In seeking to live it, we make it true. We make the ideal real. Imagination is the beginning of a different level of reality, just as the imaginal cells are the beginning of a new kind of creature.

And then, of course, there is the story we tell ourselves about ourselves. Perhaps this story began when you were a child, too young to question it. It may have told you you are not up to scratch, not getting the best marks, not as good as your sister. You may have grown up looking in the mirror and not liking what you saw. You may have so internalised these false stories that you began to *become* them. The inadequacy story may have grown arms and legs, becoming, for example, the story of 'I couldn't possibly do a job like that', or 'I was never any good with practical things, or maths, or children, or whatever else', or 'I'm no good at personal relationships, so it's better not to try'.

Ancient scripture suggests that 'as a person thinks so s/he becomes'. It matters very much indeed which stories become the narrative of our lives. Those stories will shape our minds and determine who we are becoming. We need to be aware of them and of their power, as we embark on our journey into flight.

Which stories are shaping us today?

What personal stories are shaping who you are? Do you want to keep on believing them? Might there be better, truer stories about who you are that would inspire you rather than diminishing you?

Which of our shared stories are engendering love and compassion? Which are engendering hatred, distrust and bigotry?

How could/should we change them, to bring a different kind of future into being?

A TALE OF TWO FUTURES

'*It was the best of times, it was the worst of times, it was the age of wisdom, it was the age of foolishness, it was the epoch of belief, it was the epoch of incredulity ...*'.

These are the famous opening words of Charles Dickens' novel *A Tale of Two Cities*. They could very appropriately apply to us today – in our personal struggles to make sense of all that is happening around us, in our collective and national response to the challenges opening up like a chasm ahead of us, and in our world, with all its hopes and dreams and desperation.

It feels like the worst of times – certainly as I look back over seven decades on this planet, in my own country, and in the wider world, it seems like the worst of anything I can remember. And yet there is a flicker of faith – not just conventional religious faith for that too is floundering, but a deeper and perhaps even more authentic faith in the goodness and resilience of the human spirit, inspired, as I believe it is, by a spirit greater than our own, that whispers: What if this could also be the best of times? What if, in our present times, we find ourselves in the crucible of change where a new and much more fully human future is being forged? The stars are most clearly visible in the deepest darkness. The butterfly emerges out of the worst meltdown of the chrysalis. What if these times are seen, in hindsight, to be the best of times?

It feels like the age of foolishness, when insanity is running the show, when world-changing decisions are taken by a largely uninformed or, worse, deliberately mis-informed, electorate. An age in which the most trivial of trivial pursuits seem to dominate our consciousness, while issues of enormous importance are left largely un-discussed, and unchallenged even in our parliaments. Could this ever be an age of wisdom? Wisdom is not the product of higher education, important though that may be. It is what grows when we reflect on our experience and learn from it. The more extreme and extended the experience, the greater the possibility of deeper wisdom emerging from it. The elders in our society, those who have lived longest and seen most, are, if they have also lived reflectively, the richest seam of wisdom in our society. It might be time to release them from the box we call 'frail elderly' and pay attention to what they will share with us, if only we will listen. The age of wisdom may depend on the wisdom of age. Let us not marginalise it.

It would be hard to say whether we feel we are in an age of belief or an age of scepticism. As in Dickens' time, perhaps we are in both. The age of belief, in which many of us grew up, would certainly appear to have gone. Traditional religious belief has come under serious scrutiny and traditional religious practice, at least in the western world, is in steep decline. The confidence we once had in our political leaders, and in those who were, in our youth, considered to be the 'pillars of society' has been greatly eroded, not least because of manifest misconduct, deception and abuse in high places. And yet our young people unquestioningly entrust the details of their private lives to social media sites, and there is a trust in the 'voice of the people' which has led to some potentially very damaging results. We still believe, it appears, but in what, exactly are we placing our trust in these challenging times, in which astonishingly blind belief runs hand in hand with deep scepticism and suspicion? This insane mingling of trust and distrust is nowhere more apparent than in the erosion of the value of truth in our times, and its displacement by 'post-truth', 'alternative facts' and 'fake news'.

One thing is clear in these stormy waters. We all know that the ordinary person, struggling to stay afloat in the swirling currents, feels impotent to do anything at all to change things. It is out of this sense of personal helplessness that this book is written. It suggests something very simple, but potentially world-changing. And it's something not only that each of us is *able* to engage with, but, if we think about it, morally *obliged* to engage with.

It is about the choice between two futures.

Almost inevitably we settle into the assumption that the future is in control of us, and will unfold in its own way without our being able to do much about it. What if it were the other way round? What if the future will become what we choose to make it? What if it will unfold in ways that will be shaped by the choices we make, both individually and collectively? Of course one person's choice for the best possible course in a particular situation isn't going to change the way the world works. But a million choices for the better way most certainly will. What's more, choosing the best, most life-giving course is definitely contagious. Each of us, and indeed each choice we make, can be the tipping point that shifts society from a destructive to a creative course, from a path of hatred and distrust into a path of kindness and compassion. One choice makes a difference…

Choices develop into habits.
Habits gradually shape attitudes.
Attitudes, over time, form character.

This progression is true, I suggest, both in our personal journey through life, but also in the way our society, our nation, our world evolves. We can't individually, change the character of our society, or the attitudes it exhibits. We can only attend to our own choices. If 'democracy' means anything, in what some might say is becoming a post-democratic world, it means that our choices as individuals, have value. Indeed, our choices *express* our personal values, and, it follows, the values that we would hope that our society as a whole would live by.

What do we wish the *character* of our future to be – the character of our nation, the character of our society?

What *attitudes* do we observe in ourselves, our nation and our world right now, that are continually forming our character, and the character of our society, and how do we feel about what we see there?

What *habitual ways* of thinking, speaking and acting are feeding attitudes we actually deplore, and which of them are nourishing the attitudes we truly value?

Which *choices* are we making, day by day, and what kind of mental and spiritual habits are they forming?

It really matters, how we choose, and what values guide our choosing. 'Choosing' is the only thing we can do. Far from being marginal to the state of the world, it is the one thing that is supremely important. Every choice has consequences. Those consequences will form the foundation stones for the future we desire.

Learning to live more intentionally with regard to our choices is simple. It's basically about choosing the best direction in a given situation, guided by our deepest spiritual values. But it's also very difficult, because there are so many incentives and pressures to choose less than the best. My hope is that Part 2 of this book might offer a few pointers to help us choose a better way for our own future and the future of all who come after us.

There can be little doubt that the human family is facing very real dangers from some of the movements that are sweeping through our countries. It has never been more crucial for ordinary people to steer a true course towards a future for all creation and for the planet itself that truly reflects the best that we are capable of becoming.

How would we even begin to respond to such a challenge?

In Part 2 of this handbook we will explore some possible approaches to this great work that beckons us. But first, a rather broader view of what spiritual evolution might mean, from a prophetic palaeontologist, one of the many imaginal cells of his time who was silenced in his own lifetime and speaks all the more clearly to us in ours ....

TOMORROW, ACCORDING TO TEILHARD

Before we embark on the practical work of this book, I invite you to spend a little time with a man who passed most of his adult life stretched painfully astride the gulf, as it was then, between religion and science.

I could say that I 'met' this man in a very meaningful way in 2004 during the first of many visits to the USA. The friends I was staying with in upstate New York invited me to join them on a mystery tour. The only clue they would give me about our destination was that it involved the CIA. A visit to the CIA, as may be imagined, did not strike me as a fun day out, but I concurred with rather less than good grace. We travelled up the Hudson River until we reached Hyde Park and the Culinary Institute of America (CIA), where my anxieties dissolved in a haze of anticipation of a rather special lunch, produced and served by the students of that institution.

This in itself would have been a memorable occasion, but after lunch my guide took me to the reception desk, where she was given a key to unlock the door to a secluded garden in the grounds of the Institute, which was actually a Jesuit cemetery. It was Easter, and the spring flowers were in full bloom. She led me to one little mound, absolutely covered in daffodils, and marked very simply, 'Pierre Teilhard de Chardin SJ'. It was a moment I will never forget. Teilhard is reported to have said, during a lunch date of his own with friends in 1954: 'I would like to die on the day of Resurrection.' The following year he died of a heart attack, on Easter Sunday 1955.

Fifty years separated my lunch date from his. Teilhard had died, silenced and marginalised by church authorities. His very unique imaginal cell had been thoroughly suppressed. By the time I visited his grave, however, he had become, arguably, the most informed, respected and influential communicator of the reality and possibility of spiritual evolution for our times. Out of the painful meltdown of his personal chrysalis there emerged a butterfly who would carry the human family to a much deeper understanding of what humanity is capable of becoming.

Teilhard was a scientist, a palaeontologist and a Jesuit priest, who also served in World War II as a stretcher-bearer and witnessed the worst that inhumanity can do. He was a man of deep and unshakeable faith, not only in the tenets and strictures of his own Roman Catholic tradition, but, more importantly, in the potential of human beings to rise to greater heights of consciousness and reach deeper levels of authentic humanity.

A brief overview of his thinking may be helpful to us as we seek to discern our way forward through the turmoil of our times.

Teilhard's understanding of spiritual evolution rests on the intuition that we are progressing from where we are, towards what he calls an Omega Point, the fullness of all we can be. He calls this fullness *the divine milieu*, and suggests that the universe has been following 'a certain upward trajectory' since the dawn of creation. In Christian terms we might well call this the Kingdom of Heaven of which Jesus speaks so frequently. Because he is rooted in this same Christian tradition, Teilhard sees the Christ as not just Jesus of Nazareth, but the very essence and fullness of the divine milieu – a cosmic Christ who is continually evolving, enfolding all consciousness in unimaginable wholeness, and ourselves as living cells in this evolving Body of Christ on planet Earth. By this he doesn't mean merely the signed-up church-goers or adherents to any specific faith tradition. He means all of us.

In the words of Louis Savary: 'Teilhard's spirituality is totally ecumenical, totally interfaith, and all-encompassing. Moreover, it is interplanetary and intergalactic'. Whether or not you personally would use the name 'Christ', these thoughts are worth pondering. They express the Not Yet towards which humanity is striving. They allow this consciousness to be itself evolving, and ourselves to be evolving more and more deeply into its fullness. They call us to grow beyond all the borders we have erected around our understanding of 'faith', and to live outside all the boxes we have constructed to contain it.

How does all this work? Well Teilhard describes the process as moving through four phases:

Attraction – connection – complexity – consciousness.

Attraction leads to connection, giving rise to a higher level of complexity.

We know this to be true on the human plane.

Lovers are attracted to each other; they unite, and their union may give rise to a new individual, combining their genes in a unique new manifestation of complexity.

People of like mind or common interests are attracted to each other, and connect to take their shared goals to a new level that neither or none of them could have attained individually.

Eleven people, attracted by the same game, connect with each other to form a team. No one can deny the complexity of the game of cricket, for example, that emerges from this union.

At the cellular level, single-cell organisms combine, in the course of physical evolution, to form multi-cell organisms of higher complexity. When this evolutionary process reaches a certain point, specifically in *homo sapiens*, the next stage is reached – an altogether higher level of consciousness in human beings capable of reflecting on their origins and destiny and their place in an unfolding universe. For Teilhard it seems obvious that this evolving process is a continuing one, drawing humanity towards ever higher levels of consciousness.

Evolution, he suggests always follows the direction from separateness to union, from complexity to higher complexity, from consciousness to higher consciousness, from matter to spirit. It is all about transformation, bringing into being a new state that the previous states could never have imagined. For example, hydrogen and oxygen atoms are attracted, and combine to create the more complex and hitherto unimaginable state of water. Ultimately water becomes the catalyst for life itself on this planet, and for all that follows as a result.

In this process nothing is static. It is either e-volving or de-volving, emerging or regressing. Neutrality is not an option. Every choice we make is contributing either to evolution/emergence or devolution/regression. (Note that by 'devolution' we are not talking about the desirability or otherwise of patterns of devolved government giving autonomy to separate nations, as, for example in the United Kingdom, but rather those tendencies and movements that are working against the direction of evolution in general, for example in expressions of regressive nationalism and xenophobia.)

The key to why all this matters so much lies in that assertion that every choice we make will affect the direction, either positively or negatively, towards growth or diminishment of the divine milieu, or 'the Kingdom of Heaven'. Incidentally, many people today find the word 'Kingdom' unhelpful, with its overtones of patriarchy and imperialism. Some, very helpfully, use the term 'kin-dom' instead. This change would surely resonate with Teilhard, for it expresses more truly the dynamic of attraction and interconnection as the driving force of evolution.

This still leaves us with the question of how to actually engage with this process. Teilhard suggests that we contribute to the process (or detract from it) both in what we do and in what happens to us. He defines these as our *activities* (what we do) and our *passivities* (what happens to us). In both of these experiences we can either build up or diminish the kin-dom. The questions we need to keep always in mind are these:

- What is helping me personally, and all creation to grow towards the emergence of greater fullness of life?

- What is diminishing my growth and the growth of all creation and impeding the emergence of greater fullness of life?

- What are my personal aims, ideals, dreams, desires and needs, and how well or poorly do they fit with the aim or purpose of the emerging fullness? Do I feel called to adjust any of them in the light of my observations?

- What am I learning from what happens to me, and how will I choose my attitude towards it?

Viktor Frankl in *Man's Search for Meaning* reminds us that there is one freedom that can never be taken from us, and that is the freedom to choose our attitude to any given event or situation. This conviction allowed him to retain his own essential freedom while incarcerated in a concentration camp, so it really does have the ring of authenticity.

I think Teilhard would have understood our present concerns about the state of the world and the folly of some of its leaders. In 1933, we hear, he was perturbed by the situation in Europe, calling it 'a modern human crisis'. I wonder whether he might have said the same about our global crisis now. The drumbeat of nationalism is rumbling through some of our streets and hate crime lurks in dark corners as well as parading itself in broad daylight, while the heavy footfall of religious and political fundamentalism is trampling authentic human spirituality and freedom with its dangerous dogmatism. At the same time some of the most powerful nations value economic and military supremacy more highly than the health and survival of the planet itself, and remain in determined denial about the reality and immediacy of climate change.

A few years later, in 1939, that darkest of years, however, Teilhard was also able to write: 'There is something great happening in the world ... I am not speaking of politics ... everywhere I find evidence of new beliefs and a spiritual evolution in the world.' This was a man who could be in the darkest heart of the chrysalis meltdown and truly recognise the butterfly that would emerge from it. These are the words of a true imaginal cell!

I think Teilhard would have urged us to read the signs of our own times – to recognise and react against the strident voices that incite us to hatred and conflict, but also to observe the many ways in which ordinary human beings are contributing to 'something great that is happening' in our chrysalis. He would have known, better than we, that human beings can rise to sublimity, but can also sink into depravity. We all share in the privilege of helping humanity rise to all it can be. We all share the responsibility of preventing the opposite.

If you are interested in the thinking of this man you might like to explore his works for yourself. However it cannot be denied that his writing is not easily accessible. A very helpful contemporary guide to the work and thinking of Teilhard is the former Jesuit Louis M. Savary, especially in his excellent book *The Divine Milieu Explained* (Paulist Press, 2007).

THE ART OF
MAKING CHOICES

We make millions of choices in the course of our lives, but it is equally true to say that our choices make *us*.

'*It is our choices, Harry, that show what we truly are.*' (J. K. Rowling, *Harry Potter and the Chamber of Secrets*)

My choices are revealing the truth about who I truly am, and making me what I shall become. All our choices, collectively, are shaping who we are becoming as a human race, or the inhabitants of a particular country.

What do you think about what is being shown to us so far in our choices? What might we want to adjust in the way these choices are shaping the people we are becoming?

These are the questions this book invites you to explore. It follows, then, that some help in actually making wiser choices could be very beneficial.

As in any human endeavour, there are many different approaches we might take. In one short book there is no space for more than a brief look at one particular set of guidelines, and because I have personally been formed mainly within the Christian tradition, and, within that tradition, very much influenced by the spirituality of St Ignatius Loyola, I offer you, at the beginning of this 'working journey' some of the wisdom from that tradition that has been especially helpful to me, in trying to navigate my way through the muddle and confusion in which we are currently mired. This is in no way to diminish the many other pathways to wisdom that humankind has pioneered through the ages.

Although Ignatius lived over 500 years ago, and was formed within a tradition that was facing the very necessary changes being forced by the Reformation, his insight into psychology remains today little less than cutting edge. But for our purposes you don't even need to know his name, let alone the full extent of his writings. What he can do for us here and now, and the reason for including him here in the preamble to our own journey into the future is this: his insights into ways of making wiser choices remain as valid and powerful today as they were in his own times – and it's worth remembering that his own times were also deeply troubled, his contemporaries, like us, savagely divided by the political, social and religious currents of the time.

He calls it *discernment*. If that word strikes terror into your heart, or brings down an impenetrable curtain of mystery, be reassured: *discernment* just means making wiser choices. Whatever we call it, the art of making wiser choices is going to be absolutely key in our quest to evolve spiritually. Remember, the invitation is to *grow* into the future, not to be pushed into it by any of the political, religious and social juggernauts that seem to be hogging the road.

It begins where we are. On our own we can't change the choices being made in Brussels or London or Washington. We can only change the choices we make ourselves in our own circumstances and situations. But don't under-estimate the power inherent in those personal choices. Imagine this scenario: A flock of birds is flying across the sky. All at once there is a change. Notice how just a very few of the birds strike out in a new direction. Not a radically different flight path, but sufficiently different to take the entire flock to a different destination. For those few birds that dare to make such a change it's a huge risk. They could be wrong. And even if they are not wrong, and their intuition that there is a better way is sound, the others may not follow. They may find themselves literally out on a limb. Or, as is more often the case, the rest of the flock notices this change, and chooses to follow. Gradually the direction of the whole flock is adjusted. You could say that the few pioneers of the new direction are like the imaginal cells in the butterfly story. They sense the future that is already present within them, and their great desire is to take the flock with them to a different kind of future. Which is simply to say that change usually begins with one or two pioneering spirits.

Anthropologist Margaret Mead puts it like this:

> 'Never doubt that a small group of thoughtful, committed citizens can change the world; indeed, it's the only thing that ever has.'

Those few imaginal cells who struggled for their survival inside the caterpillar were a small beleaguered group in the beginning, but it was they who carried the seeds of transformation. It always is. Never doubt the power inherent in your own choices. But along with power comes responsibility – the responsibility to choose wisely and to choose well.

Before you embark on your journey through Part 2 of this book, you might find these general questions helpful, as you reflect on any choices currently engaging you, and in considering some of what might lie ahead.

- In this situation, what is the more loving, the more life-giving thing to do next?

- Of the many options open to me, which is most likely to lead to an *increase* of love, trust, hope and understanding in myself and in the wider world? Will any of the available options *diminish* the store of love, hope and peace in myself and in the wider world?

- How will my choice affect others as well as myself – for example, my family, my community, my neighbourhood, my nation, my nation's neighbours, our world, and the whole of creation, including all the living creatures who share their planet with us?

- Will this choice tend to lead me and all creation a little closer to the best version of humanity, or could it pull us back from this fullness? Is it, primarily, an e-volutionary or a de-volutionary choice, a choice that nourishes growth or a choice tending towards regression?

- In this decision am I being mainly influenced by the hope of short term benefits or am I open to the bigger picture? When making big decisions, indigenous peoples consider the impact on 'the seventh generation'. How will my choice affect generations still unborn?

- Do I feel inwardly at peace with my choice, in my own 'gut reaction' and also in the light of the wider questions raised above?

Our personal choices have far-reaching consequences. The Butterfly Effect applies: small changes in initial conditions can have a huge impact further down the line. A slight change of air pressure in Asia can, through feedback loops, cause a hurricane in Mexico. One apparently small choice in our personal lives can affect the way humanity moves forward, or slips back, in our collective growth into the future.

Part 2 now invites you to reflect on where we find ourselves in the various stages of the metamorphosis from caterpillar to butterfly – in the growth from humanity today towards Humanity's Tomorrow – and what choices we will make in these situations in the light of how we most desire humanity to evolve into the future.

It comprises five sections, corresponding to the main stages of metamorphosis, and offering a structure for potential group reflection over several weeks. Each section offers 'conversation starters' to act as a catalyst for further thought and discussion around the personal, the global and the spiritual implications of the material.

May you journey wisely, and journey well.

PART 1
THE DREAMING SPACE

'There is nothing in a caterpillar that tells you it's going to be a butterfly.'

Margaret Fuller

WHAT FUTURE ARE
WE DREAMING?

The caterpillar journey begins with the laying of an egg. The egg is smaller than a pinhead, yet it holds within it all the potential that will ever become the caterpillar, and the butterfly. Crucially, it also contains the imaginal cells. These cells already hold the components of the future butterfly – the *imago*, the very particular butterfly that this particular caterpillar will become. The future is already held and cherished within the egg from the moment it is laid by the parent butterfly, on the perfect kind of leaf to nourish its hatching.

You too began your human journey as a single fertilised cell, almost invisible to the naked eye. In your earliest beginning you were already provided for and cherished, implanted in the place where you could grow in safety and be nourished with exactly the right kind of food until you were ready to be born. You already contained within yourself the unique person you were born to become.

Planet Earth can tell a similar story. Our home is a Goldilocks planet, where conditions were not too hot, not too cold, but just right for life to emerge over the aeons. In fact, as astrophysics now reveals, our entire universe is a Goldilocks universe, where many different parameters come together in just the right way to create the right conditions for galaxies to form and, ultimately, for a planet such as ours to evolve where life might be sustained.

The caterpillar story is just a tiny microcosm of this

overarching truth, but the message is the same. The conditions in the material universe, and especially on this planet, seem to favour the evolution of life. The universe seems to be with us, and not against us.

Although the egg is so minute, it is part of a long continuum of the human story. You belong to that bigger story. All that has gone before you – your own ancestors, and all the aeons of evolution of the human being, are your inheritance. You were born into the world standing on giants' shoulders. Not just your physical presence in the world, but, perhaps even more importantly, your spiritual presence, has been evolving through the millennia. To evolve spiritually is to move towards the best possible version of who we can be. You are invited to become the best possible you. All of us together are invited to become the best possible version of humanity.

Given this propitious beginning, and in the light of all that has passed in the human story since *homo sapiens* first emerged on planet Earth, we now find ourselves at a point where we can, together, look back to our origins and forward to our destiny and ask ourselves: What kind of a future do we desire?

Yet our experience of living in this world also shows us how incomplete this journey still is. You may find it quite hard to believe in any kind of progress, especially in our own very troubled times. Perhaps you are also asking yourself whether we really are evolving at all.

IS HUMANITY REALLY GOING ANYWHERE?

Just take a moment to be still and reflect on how you feel about the possibility of human spiritual evolution. Does it sound like a pipe dream to you? Or could it be something you would want to strive towards?

It might help to look back over a few decades, and notice some things that truly have become better, more human, more closely aligned with the sacred mystery. For example, if you look back fifty years, how was the world then? How aware were we then of our responsibility to cherish the planet we all call home? How open and tolerant were we in our attitudes to people of other faiths, other lifestyle choices, other races? How much did we care then about world poverty, and what, if anything did we do about alleviating it? What were our attitudes to war, and the use of violence to settle disputes?

If it helps, make a list of those aspects of being human that you feel are showing signs of progress towards a better way of being alive on this planet. Then make a list of any areas of life where you feel we are regressing.

If you are working in a group, bring your findings to the next meeting and share your responses.

Now look at your own personal journey. Where has there been spiritual growth in your life? Can you see the evidence of evolutionary progress in yourself? What attitudes do you notice that seem to be nourishing your growth towards a better version of yourself? Are there any underlying attitudes that you detect in yourself that are militating *against* such growth?

Examples of growth indicators might include:

- Any experience you have had of feeling more deeply open to the presence of the unseen wholeness, and holiness, of the universe, for example, in a deep relationship with another person or with the natural world, or in some personal spiritual awakening that has in any way changed the way you live your life.

- Any feelings of deep gratitude, expressions of generosity, or reaching out in compassion to another living being.

- Any time when you have experienced, or offered, the gift of genuine listening and exchange of views, possibly with someone with whom you have deep differences.

Examples of negative attitudes that could be causing you to regress might include:

- Any underlying resentments, unreasonable anger, or areas of unresolved conflict with another person or group.

- Any prejudices you may be harbouring, perhaps still unacknowledged.

- Any feelings of envy, or destructive fear, or a desire to dominate others.

- Any tendencies to live always in the past or the future but never in the present moment.

Just notice what you find, without judging yourself or anyone else. Are there any items in the lists that you feel apply to you? What might you need to add, from your own self-knowledge, either to the harvest of growth signs or the presence of negative indicators?

There is one thing you can do with these various tendencies. Like plants and weeds in your garden you can choose whether to water them or not. Imagine them as little seedlings that you can either nourish or starve, or, if necessary, pull out by the roots. You nourish them by giving them your attention and energy. You starve them by depriving them of your attention and energy. What you nourish will grow. What you starve will shrink. Which aspects of your own personality do you want to grow and which would you rather shrink?

Now take these thoughts into a wider context.

Which attitudes in our society are helping us to grow into a better version of humanity?

Which attitudes are tending to de-humanise us?

A very obvious example is to be found, regrettably, in some sections of our media – the press, television, and social media. How often have you complained about the way the newspapers report what is happening in our world? Some, it has to be said, are notoriously worse than others in turning news reporting into shameless and malicious propaganda, which ultimately undermines the very root of democracy by deliberately mis-informing the public. A simple way to counteract this negative potential is to withdraw your attention from such media outlets. You don't have to buy or read those newspapers. Your television has an OFF switch. If any social media platforms are grinding you down, you are free to disconnect.

A less tangible, but even more damaging movement is the growing freedom some people and institutions seem to have appropriated in our society today to vilify and abuse others, both physically and verbally. The increase in reported hate crime following the EU referendum in the UK was a shaming reminder of how much prejudice and bigotry lurks beneath the surface of a society that in general prides itself on being civilised and tolerant. Similar waves of intolerant and abusive behaviour have swept through other nations. They are fuelled by the violent and extreme rhetoric of some of our political leaders.

There is a direct connection between violent language and violent acts – between parliamentarians who throw vitriolic insults at their opponents and violent offenders who throw acid in the faces of their victims – between the inflammatory headlines of disreputable newspapers and the abusive hate posts that circulate in social media. Words that leave our lips or our laptops have lives of their own. They may do damage that we never intended. They may bring blessing that we never imagined.

On the positive side, there are great movements abroad that are making us *more* human: for example, the extent and success of appeals to the generosity of ordinary people, who give not only of their resources but often also of themselves, to help others in difficult circumstances. There is a determination on the part of most thinking people to work to combat climate change as far as it is being caused by our own actions and decisions, and to care for and cherish all the other life forms that share our planetary home. There is an increasing realisation that no problem is ever going to be resolved by violence, and a widespread opposition to the build-up of weaponry. These are just some of the many, many ways in which there is evidence of growth.

Just as with our more personal growth/regression tendencies, we can choose, in our society, to give our attention to all that is helping us become more fully human, and withdraw our attention from anything that is tending to dehumanise us – though in the latter case we may sometimes need to be more proactive in working *against* such tendencies, weeding them out before they spread any further.

Jodi Picoult (in *The Storyteller*) suggests:

> *Inside each of us is a monster; inside each of us is a saint. The real question is which one we nurture the most, which one will smite the other…. You cannot separate good and evil cleanly. They are conjoined twins, sharing a single heart.*

How do you feel about this suggestion?

CATERPILLAR WAYS

Wherever we are going we begin where we are. We may not much like where we are. Right now where we are doesn't look too good at all, with our world in such a state of upheaval.

The caterpillar doesn't have these worries. Worry is the flip side of the gift of conscious self-awareness. The good side is that we are able to take a long and honest look at where we are, and make adjustments to how we move forward. The caterpillars can help us.

Life in caterpillar world is in many ways a reflection of life in our own world and our own times. There are some aspects of caterpillar life that might cause us to think deeply about our own way of being on planet Earth. Try to approach this exercise with an open mind. Remember the words of Rabbie Burns: 'O wad some Power the giftie gie us/To see oursels as ithers see us!' Maybe the caterpillars can give us such a gift, if we are really open to receive it.

What might we see in this mirror?

Caterpillars are complacent. They don't get it that there could be any other life beyond their own. Their vision is limited to the next meal on the next leaf. They have no idea of the mystery they are carrying within themselves.

They are reckless consumers, chewing their way through every leaf they find, regardless of the effect this is having on the wider world.

They eat so much that they keep growing out of themselves and have to keep shedding skins to accommodate their mass.

They need to do this around five times, and they increase their body mass by as much as a thousand-fold before they eventually stop eating.

However, on the positive side:

Caterpillars hatch from eggs that were laid on just the right kind of leaf they will need to survive. They are 'goldilocks grubs'. Providence is looking out for them.

They already contain the imaginal cells that will eventually become the butterfly that each particular caterpillar is destined to become.

They do, however, have a problem with their own future. Their immune system regards the imaginal cells as aliens and goes to considerable lengths to suppress them.

What does all this have to do with us and the way we are living our lives, at least in the affluent West? What does caterpillar life reveal about how we might take stock of where we are, and what might be our first steps towards the future we desire?

You might like to consider these questions:

How limited do we feel is our vision of life – our nation's vision? Does the word 'complacent' apply at all to the way we handle the pressing issues of our times – for example the refugee crisis, or the way we relate to those who are strangers in our midst? How self-centred are we in our personal relationships? How do we feel about the prevalent 'Me first' or, more commonly, 'My nation first' philosophy? How does this attitude fit in a world where no one of us and no one of our nations can truly flourish at the expense of others? How does it fit with the teaching of all our spiritual traditions that we are all brothers and sisters, whichever nation we call home, and that we are enjoined to treat each other as we wish others to treat us?

Do we recognise in ourselves and our society the habit of reckless consumption? How mindful are we of the effect of our consumption on the planet that sustains us? Are we taking an unfair share of the world's resources, and depriving other peoples and other life forms of their rightful needs? Are there any ways in which we could effectively simplify our lives?

Are we expanding so much, in our perceived needs and expectations, that we are literally growing out of ourselves? For example, how realistic are our expectations of our health care system? Are we demanding more and more services that risk leaving others deprived? Are we developing an attitude of entitlement to all the good things of life, even though this clearly deprives others of such benefits? Resources, as the caterpillars discover, are not limitless. What does love ask of us in these circumstances?

How do we respond to the prophetic voices of our times, even, and especially, when their message is uncomfortable? Whose are these voices? They may be high profile figures, warning us, for example, of the imminence of climate change, or simply the person next door who is living her life in a way that challenges us to think more deeply about our own priorities.

Do we want our future on this planet to follow the Caterpillar Model? Are we content to be such a consuming, ego-centric presence on our planet? So far, caterpillar thinking has shaped our politics, and this is especially in evidence in our present times. But we are not permanently locked in to a caterpillar existence unless this is what we choose. Do we really believe that the seed of the best person we can become is already present in our own hearts? Do we trust our own imaginal cell? Do we believe the words of ancient wisdom that assure us that 'the treasure is within you'? The caterpillar story really does confirm this.

WORKING TOGETHER? PULLING APART?

One of the most heartbreaking consequences of the UK's narrow decision (by 37.4 per cent of the registered electorate and 51.9 per cent of the actual votes cast) to withdraw from the European Union, has been the overnight change from an atmosphere of friendly co-operation with our European neighbours, to an adversarial, competitive stance. We ceased to be one among 28 countries trying, with varying degrees of success, to work together for the greater good, to being 1 against 27 countries, seeking the best competitive advantage for ourselves.

The hostile rhetoric from some of our politicians that accompanied this change, has been shaming, and deeply painful to millions of people in the UK and across the whole continent of Europe whose lives are inter-connected in families, or as friends or colleagues with those in other EU countries, and who in no way wish it to be otherwise. Where until recently we have all been striving to work together, we are now being pulled apart.

Apart. The word is loaded.

My eight-year-old granddaughter was working on a project about South Africa, her father's homeland. As she was telling me about it, she stumbled over the word *apartheid*. I realised that she didn't actually know what it meant. I tried to explain to her that the people of South Africa were a bit like the keys on a piano – some black, some white, some dark-skinned, others light-skinned and that the policy of apartheid had separated them in every practical way, privileging the white-skinned people and cruelly oppressing the dark-skinned. When she thought about the piano analogy, it was immediately obvious to her that if you were to separate out one colour of keys, you would destroy the music. She also got it, straight away, that if you separate out one group of people from a community, both the community itself, and those who have been set apart, will be damaged and diminished. The fullness of the human music will be compromised.

Ultimately humanity is destined for deeper unity. Forces that pull us apart are working *against* that destiny, whether this happens in the political, or the social, or the religious arena. Competition sets us against each other. Co-operation draws us closer together. But there is a third way. Recently a new word has been coined: *coopetition*.

I first came across this concept when an American high school teacher told me about an international contest in which some of his pupils took part. The contest was to design and build a robot. There were several prizes, but the main prize did not go to the team who constructed the best robot. It went to the team who demonstrated the greatest willingness to help those in other, competing, teams if they encountered a problem. Competing, in this friendly way, to achieve the highest possible level of co-operation sounded to me like a brilliant way of proceeding in the quest for human evolution – something worth dreaming about.

This reminded me of the story of the children's Sports' Day in a school that catered for able-bodied children and for those with special needs. The children with various challenges had a running race of their own, but it took an unexpected course. Halfway along the track one of them stumbled and fell over.

Without a moment's hesitation every child in that race turned back to help their unlucky classmate. They then linked hands and completed the race together, crossing the finishing line as one. It is said that the parents and teachers gave them a standing ovation. Those children had shown, in their simple unanimous act of solidarity, that it is far more important to live true to our humanity, than to win a medal, or to get a good trade deal.

The traditional exhortation in marriage ceremonies, 'What God has joined, let not man put asunder', can still serve us well. Regardless of whether you believe human alliances, including the marriage alliance, are divinely engineered, the wisdom remains valid: let us not, in our short-sighted and egocentric desire to pursue our own advantage, whether personal or national, pull apart the deeper fibres of humanity that bind us together.

The imaginal cells can help us here. They start life as separate entities, and over time discover each other, and begin to resonate together. The caterpillar's immune system initially works to prevent this, by subduing them and keeping them infantile. Yet the course of evolution will not be undermined. Inevitably when the time is right they will come together to bring forth the future butterfly and when that time comes, the caterpillar cells that were so hostile towards them will become the soup that nourishes them. Competition will yield to co-operation.

When I was first learning primary school maths, we called division sums 'sharing'. Now I know better. When we come together to share our gifts and resources, the result is addition and multiplication. When we pull apart, each pursuing our own ends, the result is subtraction and division.

And our own end is exactly what we will discover.

DREAMING A BIGGER STORY

T imes of crisis change the story. The narrative we have been
living by can be called into question. Take the caterpillars:
their narrative is all about caterpillars and how to make the
forest best serve their needs. Part of that story is the need to
keep the imaginal cells down, so that they don't rock the boat.
When the crisis comes the story changes. Opposition becomes
co-operation. A different story warns them that if they want to
live they will have to let themselves die, and in a rather nasty way,
in the chrysalis. After the struggle to emerge from the chrysalis,
the butterfly then begins life in a different story again – a story
about nectar and pollen – the giving and taking in a mutually
life-giving relationship – a story about flight and migration and
an inter-generational collaboration

The stories we live by change as we ourselves change. The
longer we live, and reflect on our lives, the wider our horizons
extend, and we need a bigger story, one that resonates with our
actual experience. We may discover that the stories we lived by as
children no longer ring true to us, or no longer match our adult
observation. For example, when you were a child you may have
been told that 'every time you tell a lie a fairy dies'. This was a 'small
story'. You soon grew out of it. But as you grew older you realised
that a bigger, universal story underpins the fairy story, which warns
us that every time we are untruthful or dishonest, we damage

something important in the invisible network of humanity that holds us together. We may all too easily dismiss the small stories as the outgrown stuff of childhood. We may not recognise the bigger story until we are ready to let go of the smaller stories and yet the small stories also held important seeds of truth.

But before we adjust our stories, it's important to distinguish between the really big stories that guide us, and remain consistent throughout all the changing scenes of life, and those more personal stories that grow and change as we do. More than at any time that I can remember in my own lifetime, we need to know where we stand with the stories, and to recognise the difference between those that are enduring and universal and those that are subject to modification in the light of experience.

The big stories express the values we desire to live by, and to embody in our ways of governing ourselves and relating to each other. They hold good from one generation to the next, unless some programme of mass indoctrination derails them. Something like this is perhaps the equivalent of a mutation in the genetic code. The eruption of a brutal regime, for example, changes the course of human history, but also challenges all that is best in us to find a new direction together, beyond the killing fields. But the deeper stories endure. They even hold good across all the artificial borders that politics and religion may erect between the peoples of the earth.

Perhaps I can share a couple of my own 'growing and changing' stories.

During the first seven years or so of my life I had no exposure at all to organised religion. I was an only child, and played freely in the woods adjoining our little home. I knew then beyond any shadow of doubt that 'God' (though I wouldn't be able to define that term, either then or now) lived in the woods. This conviction took root in my heart and developed into my lifelong conviction that the divine is present in every aspect of the natural world, including ourselves, even in me, a six-year-old child.

Then at age seven or so I was sent to Sunday School, and although I cherish what was given to me then in the form of the traditional Christian story, it was a shock to hear, through the church (mainly in the hymns and liturgies), that I was actually 'fallen' and in need of salvation, though it was by no means clear what I had done to warrant this change of status. The necessary 'salvation', I was taught, depended on a ritualised blood sacrifice, and could only be administered through the offices of the ecclesiastical institution and its designated ministers. Any transgression on my part would jeopardise my eternal future. Now, with six decades of hindsight, I have come to question this second story and to grow beyond it. But the 'God in all things' narrative that I learned in the woods is as eternal to me now as it was then. It is the deeper narrative that I live by.

Another story I was told in those early years was passed on to me by my Victorian great-aunt (born 1880, therefore genuinely 'Victorian'). In my childhood the map of the world was dominated by pink, marking the extent of the British Empire. I recall her telling me one day how grateful I should be that I was born British. I never questioned it then. But about fifteen years later when I was living and working in Berlin, I was reminded of my aunt's comment when a German colleague asked me whether it was a source of regret to me that I wasn't born German. Those two comments, juxtaposed, made me smile, and perhaps that was the beginning of a long process of asking what identity really means, and, especially, what national identity really means. They also pose difficult questions about whether any nation state with very questionable history and some shamefully dark periods in its story really has the moral right to claim our uncritical fidelity.

Now in our present turmoil, which story is a story to live by? Now I can see that Victorian 'patriotism' was a small story which I have, frankly outgrown, as I have, I hope, matured into a world citizen as well as a resident of my own homeland. Now, quite possibly, my grandchildren have never even heard of the British Empire. That story has become history. Now as we are increasingly facing questions about who we really are and where we really belong, many are realising that national identity is a layered phenomenon. By moving around our world, living, working and forming life relationships across national borders, we are growing into a bigger story, a post-nationalist story. Only when the small tribal story rises up and attempts to derail the bigger story do we begin to realise just how much is at stake here. This, I suspect, is what is happening now.

So what is this 'bigger story'? I would suggest that it is now a story not about national boundaries or about religious demarcations, but about shared *values* and the human experience we all have in common. What are the fundamental human values that we share and what story are they giving us to live by? What is working against those values and what is helping them to flourish?

Let's think big on this one. So-called liberal democratic values are taking a hammering in our times, both from extreme religious fundamentalism of various shades, but also from the movements in some regions towards a right-wing, nationalist worldview. Liberal values have been unjustly yoked to what has become known as the 'liberal elite' (whoever they are) against which powerful populist movements seem to have declared war. We certainly need to be more proactive in eliminating social elitism from the way we do our politics, but if we focus on the 'liberal', what would that mean? What do ordinary human beings value, wherever in the world they live and whatever creed they may or may not espouse?

Suggestions might be:

Basic care and compassion for all, including decent housing, health care, education, social care and security, regardless of any ability to pay for these things.

An open society welcoming of the outsider, hospitable to those in need wherever they come from, especially refugees and those fleeing violence, and tolerant of opinions and life choices that may differ from our own.

Free and open communication between nations and communities so that the best we discover can be freely shared with each other, for example, scientific and medical research, and academic and cultural exchange.

Freedom of speech, lifestyle and belief, provided that this freedom fully respects the equal freedoms of others who have different opinions.

Democratic principles in international, national, local and family decisions, where each person's view is heard and respected and reasonable consensus is sought

The primacy of human values of love, compassion and justice over the lesser pursuits of economic or military supremacy. The primacy of global concerns over parochial, insular or national interests, when choices have to be made.

CONVERSATION STARTERS ...

 PERSONAL IMPLICATIONS

How much of your own standard of living would you willingly sacrifice for the sake of the wellbeing of the planet or of other less privileged peoples? For example, would you be willing to pay higher taxes to support better healthcare, social services and overseas aid?

Would you like to simplify your lifestyle? If so, can you see any practical steps you might take to achieve this?

What stories guide your life? Can you see which of these stories have an eternal, universal quality? How can you live these deep stories more fully? Which stories have changed and become irrelevant or even harmful through the years as you have grown through different stages of your life? Can you let them go if necessary?

 NATIONAL AND GLOBAL IMPLICATIONS

Would you prefer your country to be governed as a business or as a community?

What prophetic voices are disturbing your peace right now? What is disturbing your nation's peace? Which voices would you rather not hear? Are you deliberately closing them down? What is happening to such voices in your society?

What human values do you think make up the best Big Story we can all live by? Which values do you believe should prevail when we have to make collective choices?

Which do you feel is ultimately more important to the human story: competition or co-operation? How might these two instincts work together?

 SPIRITUAL IMPLICATIONS

Do you think humanity is evolving into a better version of itself? If so, where do you see the evidence for this, and how might you nourish it? What does the possibility of 'spiritual evolution' mean to you?

Wherever two or more gather there can be significant spiritual growth. Small groups of thoughtful people can move humanity forward in very important ways. This is a simple expression of the 'gathering process' in which we gradually grow beyond our smaller identity to contribute to a higher reality of what it could mean to be fully human. How could you personally contribute to this gathering process, perhaps by joining with others to explore the direction the human family is going, and where we actually want it to go?

How does your religious/spiritual tradition view spiritual evolution, and what light does it shed on our quest to become the best possible version of ourselves? How does it inspire and encourage you to dream? What does it ask of you in bringing this dream to birth?

PART 2
A WORLD IN CRISIS

'A crisis is a holy summons to cross a threshold.'

Sue Monk Kidd

WHEN THINGS ARE FALLING APART

S omething's not right in Caterpillar World. If you would like to hear more about it from the caterpillar's mouth, read the section *Disintegration* in the companion volume to this book, *Hidden Wings*. Their world is falling apart in ways that may remind us of some aspects of our own society now. What the caterpillars don't know, and can't know, is that they are going through a natural process that will lead them, sooner rather than later, into a massive meltdown as they literally dissolve into a new state – a very uncomfortable state – in the chrysalis.

As human beings our default position when going through times of serious global turmoil is to assume that this is completely bad news, and, for sure, in the short term it almost always *is* a destructive situation, from which few of us will escape unscathed. A question we might usefully ask ourselves is this: Is the experience of apparent social and political disintegration we are now going through just bad news, or might we be plunging into a period of meltdown in which new ways forward are gestating? This possibility does not just come from the caterpillars. It is a pattern we see right across the natural world, and, indeed, in our own personal experience. What appears at the time to be a painful disruption of all our certainties seems to release a new energy which in hindsight is seen to have been transformative.

However, it isn't at all easy to believe in this possibility when you are in the middle of the falling-apart. I sometimes ask myself how much proof do I need, when I see the evidence of new life springing from the breakdown of old systems almost everywhere I look. When I walk in the countryside in winter, I don't need reminding that in a few months' time it will be green again. The flowers will be coming through. The birds will sing again. But when I get stuck in my own feelings of despair about the way things are going, either in my personal journey or on the national and international scenes, I feel no such inner assurance. At such times I need to deliberately recall other times in the past when things have fallen apart, and then ask myself: Did I survive? Did I maybe even *grow*, through such experiences?

Last Easter I came across an animated internet clip that made me smile, and which, maybe I really need to internalise. It depicted a basket of ordinary-looking eggs. One after another, they were decorated in different colours and with ribbons and flowers – the whole works. Each time an egg received its decoration it gave a little cry of delight. By the time all this decorating was finished, just one egg remained, unadorned and clearly miserable The others commiserated with it, as they preened themselves in their new Easter finery.

Time passed. The naked little egg sat there and waited, unable to redeem itself from this predicament. And then came the explosion. Its shell fell apart with a resounding crash, and out came a chick. The decorated eggs reminded me of how easy it would be to think that life is all about making ourselves as prosperous and successful as possible, and basking in the satisfaction that this would bring. But what if there were more? More than the bigger house or the better trade deal? What if something completely new were waiting to emerge.

The bad news is that the chick can only emerge when the shell falls apart. Is the new possibility worth the pain of the falling apart? Conversely, when our shell is breaking, this may not just signify the shattering of our existing 'egg securities', but quite possibly the hatching of a chick – a whole new realm of possibility.

This transformation for caterpillars is, of course, the emergence of the butterfly. They have no choice, and therefore no chance of getting it wrong. For us it's different. In our chaotic breakdowns there are choices. We can, through our response to the situation, tilt the world a little bit towards serious and damaging breakdown, or a little bit towards truly creative transformation. The chrysalis time we are entering in our own day and age also holds hidden wings. But will that future become a terrible holocaust – the wings of a vulture – or an amazing breakthrough into new and better ways of being human – the wings of an angel?

I believe that the seriousness of the world situation today truly warrants this kind of language and we ignore the warning signs at our extreme peril. With this in mind, let's take a closer look at where we find ourselves and how we might most creatively respond to what we see.

DISENCHANTMENT

It would be impossible to miss the signs of deep disillusionment breaking out in many of the world's regions today, but most especially perhaps in parts of Europe and the United States. (The word 'disillusionment' doesn't even come near to describing how people must be feeling in the beleaguered countries of Africa and the Middle East.) Just as we in the western world were, metaphorically, sunning ourselves on the beaches of complacent prosperity, along came the tsunami of popular revolt, that has taken us all by storm and left us frantically searching for a foothold in the shifting political landscape. The status quo is collapsing. There is a groundswell of opinion that things can't continue as they have been, in a world where the majority of ordinary people, one way or another, feel alienated and powerless, and marginalised by their own elected leaders who, they complain with some justification, 'are just not listening'.

It reminds me of the experience of standing barefoot on the shore as the waves break on the sands. First there is the crash of the breaking wave. Then, as the water recedes, there is a suction underfoot that can carry you with it, creating a temporary vacuum and pulling part of the beach back into the ocean. We too may have the feeling of having been sucked into a power vacuum, in which the old alignments no longer hold, but the new kids on the block demonstrably can't be trusted.

In *Hidden Wings*, you may recall, the caterpillars complained that the whole infrastructure appeared to be collapsing. And certainly, if you are just discovering that things can't continue the way they have been all your life so far, but you have no idea of what might come next, you have good reason to be anxious. The same goes for us. We are told repeatedly how strong our economy is, and how safe in our leaders' 'expert' hands. And in the next news report we learn that there is no money to adequately fund our schools, hospitals, libraries or care for the elderly, or to provide support for those with disabilities, to pay for highway maintenance or to fund athletes in some Olympic sports. On the other hand there is no shortage of money for the maintenance of weapons of mass destruction, for engagement in proxy wars, and for armies of mandarins to unravel perfectly good trading arrangements with our neighbours.

Small wonder that the caterpillars on the forest floor, the ordinary people in the villages, towns and cities of our lands, are disgruntled, and even, it appears, ripe for revolt. When you disregard the growing voices of protest at the grass roots, and then you put the blunt instrument of a plebiscite into those disillusioned hands, they will hit straight back at you, regardless of what the deeper issues of the vote may have been. This, it would seem, is a large part of what has happened in the UK and the US. There is an inexorable logic about it.

In February 2017 there was an avalanche in the French Alps which tragically robbed four innocent people of their lives. The people who were killed were simply walking back from snowboarding on a regular route. The avalanche was started by two skiers jumping into the top of that route, skiing recklessly off-piste without checking that the bottom of the route was clear. This is what can happen on a grand scale in our present situation. Reckless political action at the leadership level can trigger an avalanche of potentially deadly consequences for those who are going about their regular business on the lower rungs of the social ladder. Something like this happened in the summer of 2017, when a catastrophic, but apparently completely preventable, fire in a London tower block became a flashpoint that would blow wide open the festering divisions caused by social deprivation in the UK and the effects of indifference, irresponsible cost-cutting and injustice in high places.

Yes. The caterpillars *are* disillusioned! We don't believe what our leaders say any more. We don't trust them with our future, with our children's education or our elders' welfare. We don't trust them with our health service or our economy. They have not been straight with us. They have not listened to our warnings or our cries for help. They have provided ample evidence that they have no coherent plan or any idea of how to move forward and we watch, impotently, as some of them fight like rats in a sack for positions of power. So what can we do?

Some of us are natural agitators. Some of us have agitation thrust upon us, when the burning issues begin to affect our own lives or those of our children. Personally I belong in the latter category, and I have agonised over how to react effectively to what I see happening in my own country. The normal democratic channels don't seem to be working very well, but those channels should nevertheless be the first line of action. If your elected representative stands in a very different position to your own, there is little you can do, except ply him or her with – constructive – letters and emails and rather fruitlessly use your vote every five years or so. And of course you could consider running for elected office yourself, or becoming proactive in other ways. It is very understandable, though also to be deplored, that so many of our citizens don't even go to the polls because they don't think it will make any difference. So when some radically new movement sweeps across the country or the world, it is unsurprising that many of the disillusioned eagerly, and perhaps uncritically, climb on board.

Alongside the growing discontent with the established

channels of power, however, there has been a significant growth in the power of grass-roots protest movements, such as the international *Avaaz*, or the UK-based *38 Degrees*. These movements are capable, through the use of social media, of activating mass protests on issues of social or political concern, such as climate change, the distribution of the world's resources, the protection of minorities and of the poorest of earth's peoples, action to prevent conflict, and the calling out of globalised institutions who are abusing their power. These organisations are crowd-funded and therefore, so far, free from manipulation by those with vested interests in the status quo. They operate democratically, regularly asking their supporters for their own opinions about the issues of the day and on what issues they would wish them to speak out. The fact that their very existence is being targeted and threatened by some governments and institutions is another healthy sign that they are doing something right, articulating a prophetic spirit and giving a means of expression to our imaginal cells. One thing we can do is to consider giving them our support – which means nothing more demanding in the first instance than signing up to receive their emails, and selectively signing their petitions, each of us according to our own conscience. We can choose to support them financially or not, as we see fit, with no pressure.

We are riding a stormy sea. Let's talk about what we are experiencing, and what we can do, together, to steer the ship of humanity to new horizons rather than into shipwreck.

GROWING OUT OF OURSELVES

Remember how the caterpillars increase their body mass up to one thousandfold, and shed their skins five times before they finally stop their unbridled expansion? Does this strategy reflect our own ways as human beings? I remember a book being published in 1972, *The Limits of Growth*, calling into question the received philosophy that exponential economic growth was the way forward for humanity. We are still waiting for its wisdom to be applied in our prosperous western societies, where the overriding importance of consumerism remains the ruling deity. The idea of limiting growth was an imaginal cell of its time. It is still being held in enforced dormancy.

We in the west have certainly been chewing our way through every leaf in the forest, with scant regard for the effects of our behaviour on the rest of creation. Greed has superseded need as our prime motivator. And this is about more than just material resources. The 'eat all you can get' mentality is a symptom of infancy. Infants must be allowed to be ego-centric consumers, otherwise they could not grow and thrive. As any new parent knows, a new-born takes centre stage, and screams for service, day and night. But the years pass and gradually we have to learn that we are not the centre of the larger universe. We grow up. We adapt our behaviour to take account of the legitimate needs and desires of others. Our view of life expands rapidly, from the confines of the nursery, which once we controlled with a dictator's grip, to a whole world teeming with billions of others. We grow up into the bigger picture.

Like the caterpillar we have to keep on shedding our outgrown attitudes. Nursery narcissism gives way (in most people) to a mature engagement with the requirements of *inter-dependency*, where we take our share of responsibility for the wellbeing of the whole of creation, and learn to make choices not solely guided by what's best for ourselves, but also by what best serves the greater good. It turns out, of course, as ancient wisdom has always taught us, that the two are the same. What is best for all creation is ultimately, also best for every creature.

Crucial questions in our times, therefore, would be these:

Are the personal choices we are making still being mainly driven by our egocentric toddler selves, or by the mature person who is emerging in our lives?

Are the choices we make as nations being mainly driven by what is best for ourselves and our own tribe, or do they take account of what is good for our neighbours, for the poorest and weakest of our citizens, and for the wider world?

Are the choices human beings are making collectively mainly driven by what is best for human beings, or do they also take account of what is good for the planet we all call home and for all of the natural world?

When I examine myself and my own country through this lens I am not comfortable with what I see. There would appear to be an urgent need to correct our collective course away from *Me First* and towards *All of Us Together*. And 'All' means ALL. We have some serious growing up to do if we want to evolve towards the next stage of the best version of ourselves. Our inner toddler is constantly nagging us to regress right back to the nursery. Which direction will we choose?

At times like these it can seem that everything really is winding down, starting with public services and ending with personal and national morale. But it is also true that at times like these something else is just waking up. You could call this the imaginal cell – that spirit within us that holds the possibility of the best version of ourselves – the prophetic voice that calls us beyond ourselves. Perhaps that's part of the tension that is causing us all so much pain. Faced with this level of tension, we can either retreat into ourselves and curl up, head in the sand, passively waiting for the future to unfold, or we can embrace the energy of the chrysalis, becoming birthing partners of our own future and the future of all humanity.

TRANSFORMING THE ENERGY OF BREAKDOWN

Science proposes that energy can't be created or destroyed. It can only be directed and transformed. Think of all the energy we expend in our 'caterpillar state'. All that busy-ness, that running back and forth, trying to keep all our projects in the air, multi-tasking. All the energy that goes into the best of our endeavours, our inventiveness, our creative solutions and new initiatives. Just as the caterpillars expend enormous energy chewing away at their leafy world, before collapsing into the chrysalis state, so too do we. That energy has to go somewhere, and so it is that the chrysalis state of the caterpillar's metamorphosis is the stage of maximum energy expenditure. What seems to be hanging lifelessly from a branch is in fact a high intensity butterfly factory.

This fact should give us encouragement. What may appear now to be a state of helplessness as we watch national and global events unfold around us, could in fact be a stage of human evolution where energy once used for purposes we understood and controlled, is now freed up for purposes of transformation that we don't understand at all, and yet in which we are deeply and personally involved.

Some of the energy that is absorbed into the chrysalis state is negative energy. Many people today are feeling angry, fearful and even desperate about what is happening in their world and their country. There are recriminations and an apportioning of blame, and this will surely increase dramatically as the full effects of some of our recent electoral decisions become apparent. While we can perhaps see how creative energy can become part of the transformation process, can our negative energies also be transformed?

Following an incident many years ago when I almost dispatched the typescript of my first book to a fraudulent agent who was found to be using a false address, I remember going into a slightly frenzied clean-up operation. This near-miss had generated a lot of anger and dismay in me, and, not really knowing what to do next I decided to clear out a room full of junk that had been taking up space in the house for as long as I could remember. It took me several days, but eventually that room was transformed into a rather lovely quiet space that I, and others, used for meditation. I wish I could say that I have always been able to direct my anger and frustration into creative channels. Or, indeed, that I could tell you I have discovered what to do with my present turmoil, but it was a lesson to me, that anger is also energy, and we have choices about where we direct our energy. (It also taught me that there was no need for an agent anyway.)

Helpful questions might be:

When I am angry or frustrated or hurt by something that has happened, what is my first response? I can fairly easily find someone to listen to my grumbling. There are plenty of kindred spirits around today in my own country who share my misgivings about our domestic politics. And if I were so minded I could also go online and vent my displeasure all over the internet. But if I do this, I will actually be *amplifying* the anger, not re-directing or transforming it.

In adversarial situations such as we now see in our divided

countries and communities, do I pile on the blame, and make myself feel better by vilifying those I see as the opposition? If I do this, I am only intensifying the divisions. The caterpillars have a different strategy. You may recall that the caterpillar's immune system initially fights the imaginal cells and keeps them down. But once the chrysalis meltdown has begun, all that opposition turns into co-operation. The dissolving caterpillar cells become the nutrition for the developing imaginal cells. That is *real* transformation, and it has everything to teach us.

Richard Rohr warns us that if we do not learn to transform our pain we will transmit it. In the Christian tradition we see this dynamic in action right at the heart of the faith. On the cross the negative energy is truly absorbed, and can then be transformed into the life-giving energy of the Holy Spirit, released, as Christians believe, out of the hugely destructive act of the crucifixion. We are not asked to absorb the world's pain, or even to deny our feelings of anger and resentment when life events, or other people, harm us. The invitation is to look squarely at our own experience of pain, and ask ourselves how we might redirect its negative energy into creative, rather than destructive channels.

SETTLING SPACE OR SPRINGBOARD

As soon as we begin to think of our life as a spiritual journey, an obvious question presents itself: Where are we going? What is the destination?

My ears pricked up recently during a TV nature documentary. The narrator, who was making an unhurried, contemplative river journey through southern Ireland, commented that 'If there is no time, you can't be late. If there is no destination you can't get lost'.

I can get lost in a paper bag, so the option of having no destination, and therefore no way of getting lost, is very attractive. And the more I think about it, the more appealing it becomes, to be free of the shackles of some pre-determined destination, or the tyranny of time.

The narrator then revealed that he had chosen to settle in a particularly lovely spot on the west coast of Ireland, after years of extensive travel. I too recently settled in my own little place after years of travel, and was able very much to relate to his experience. But is it realistic to live with no pre-defined destination?

The thing about a destination is that it represents a fixed point, and in reality, life, being an ever-moving target, rarely provides such a luxury. It is we who fix the end points of our endeavours. Life often overthrows such plans and calls into question any belief we ever had that there is an end point to our various journeys. Arrival at the summit of a hill, for example, when you are hiking, usually just opens up a vista of many more summits still to come. Destination after destination.

In religious traditions the destination is commonly perceived as 'heaven' – some undefined post-mortem eternal reward. This gives rise to the assumption that there are things we can do, or avoid doing, in order to obtain a passport to this destination, which in turn places enormous spiritual and emotional power in the hands of those who appoint themselves the issuing authority of these passports – those who tell us who is, and who is not, to be granted an entry visa.

So imagining a world without a pre-set destination would offer a very different backdrop to the human adventure. What if we were to replace the concept of 'destination' by the word 'destiny'. It would no longer be a question of achieving some goal determined by an external authority, like a pass mark in an examination. It would no longer be about conquering other lands or persuading other people to live their lives by our norms and values. It would no longer be about converting others to our own narrow view of the sacred mystery or imposing our own set of doctrines and practices on them. Rather, it would be about journeying more and more deeply into the destiny of who we truly are, who we are born to be, the destiny of 'becoming fully human, fully alive'. It would be about *growing up*. In this quest each one of us, and each group of us, will discover our own ways of making this journey. And because it is not a specific narrow destination, there is no possibility of getting lost, because every path that is focused on the vision of 'the human being fully alive' is a good path.

The notion of a pre-conceived destination can also seduce us into a false sense of security. My own settling space felt like a kind of destination. I thought I had arrived at a place where I could pass the remaining years of my life with a degree of comfort, familiarity and security. Yet within a few years of turning the key in the door of what I intended to be my final home, the entire landscape of my homeland has shifted, and my settling space could become an unwanted springboard, quite possibly catapulting me, for better or for worse, into quite new circumstances that I would never have desired or dreamed possible. All my assumptions about the stability and reliability of my own country's values and attitudes have been challenged during the past twelve months and my soul's habitat feels threatened. Moreover, there is a growing consensus that our entire world is going mad, nothing is impossible anymore and the worst we could fear may actually happen. I am not alone in feeling exposed and vulnerable in the very place where I expected to feel safe.

All this evokes a great deal of sympathy with the caterpillars. In the next segment of our journey we will join them as their own settled space in the forest falls apart both around them and within them – the unimaginable becomes a reality, the impossible becomes actual, the clown wears the crown and reason flees the stage. Is it the end of the world as we know it, or is it the springboard to a whole new future, whose shape we cannot begin to imagine?

The springboard, it turns out is very often some unexpected and unwanted event. A story is told of a duck that spent its days on a little pond in the park. It loved its pond. It was permanently settled there and thought it was in heaven. It thought its pond was the whole world. Then one day a crow flew overhead, noticed the duck and swooped down, seizing the startled bird and carrying it off high into the sky. Once the duck overcame its terror, it began to look at the vista spread out below. 'Oh my goodness,' it thought. 'There are other ponds in other parks. There are rivers and lakes and there is even an ocean that stretches into infinity.' Eventually the crow relented, dropped the duck and it flew back to its home pond. But the pond was never the same again, because now the duck had glimpsed a bigger reality.

CONVERSATION STARTERS ...

 PERSONAL IMPLICATIONS

When you are feeling angry or frustrated, how do you deal with these feelings? Can you see any ways in which you might direct this potentially negative energy into potentially positive channels?

Are you feeling settled? If not, in what ways do you feel your settled state is disintegrating?

Have you ever had the experience of being catapulted into a different place in your story, possibly by an adverse and unwanted event?

 NATIONAL AND GLOBAL IMPLICATIONS

What signs of crisis do you see in our world and our nations today? How is the crisis revealing itself? Towards what threshold might these signs be calling us?

Amid the evidence of breakdown in our society, where do you see the signs of positive growth? Where do you see negative movements or tendencies? What might motivate you to raise a voice of protest, and how would you go about it?

To what extent do you feel you, or your nation, are adopting a 'me first' approach to current problems? Where do you see any evidence of less ego-centric attitudes, and how could you support them?

 ## SPIRITUAL IMPLICATIONS

Is it desirable or feasible to keep on expanding on a planet with limited resources and space? For example, is year-on-year economic growth an ethical aspiration? Is the next-bigger house on the property ladder always a desirable aim? Should we trust 'market forces' to take care of the needs of the poorest among us?

What does your religious/spiritual tradition teach about growth, consumption and expansion, and the challenge to prioritise the good of all people and all creation over the demands of the ego-centre? In what ways is your religious/ spiritual tradition leading by example? What part might you be invited to play in rising to this challenge?

PART 3
OVER THE EDGE

'A part of us has to die to transform; and a part of us dies if we don't. Which part will prevail?'

Jett Psaris

TAKING THE
PLUNGE

We haven't yet gone over the edge of whatever future awaits us. In today's turmoil, there are voices telling us everything will get better as a result of some of our recent choices. Others, equally valid, are warning us that we may be about to go over the edge of a cliff. Time will tell which voices are closer to the truth. It seems certain, however, that the world is on the brink of a new stage of our evolution as human beings. It could go either way. We could be entering a period of destructive regression or we could be on the brink of an ascension to a higher level of consciousness. The outcome depends on our own personal and collective choices.

It's all a bit like sailing reasonably placidly along a river, and then suddenly coming to a waterfall on the scale of Niagara. You know that a frightening drop might lie ahead but you still have no real idea of what it could be like. It's not even clear what has brought us to this critical point. Many rivers, each becoming increasingly turbulent, seem to have converged, to plunge together over the falls: the river of global climate change; the economic crisis triggered by banking malpractices; the ecclesiastical crises following the exposure of abuse and accompanying cover-ups, leading many to abandon religious practice; the migrant crisis, bringing millions of the dispossessed and the victims of conflict to safer shores and now the mounting political crises, including those triggered by UK and US electoral events. All these, and more, have brought us to the edge. But is it the edge of catastrophe? Or is it the edge of tomorrow?

Not infrequently I have met people for whom the image of a waterfall has resonated deeply in their personal experience. Perhaps they have suffered an unexpected bereavement, or the loss of a job, of health or mobility or the breakdown of a significant relationship. Their experience has plunged them into a terrifying descent, straight over the Falls.

When you are on the river there is very little you can do to avoid the Falls into which you are heading. I remember watching the water crashing over the Minnehaha Falls in Minnesota one day and then walking on to where the river continued its post-traumatic flow. It soon became calm again, and a little further downstream I watched a family of otters swimming playfully in the gentler waters. It spoke to me of a promise that there is life beyond the Falls, but it surely doesn't feel like that when you are about to plunge to unknown depths. Another reality check about the Falls: once you have gone over the edge there is no way of climbing back up the cascade. The only way is onward. Once the die has been cast, however unwisely, the decision can normally not be reversed and we have to search for constructive ways to live with, and grow beyond, the consequences of our choices.

Amazingly, a few people have actually survived the plunge over Niagara. A seven-year-old boy once went over, to his parents' horror. He arrived at the foot of the Falls and was picked up, unharmed, by one of the *Maid of the Mist* tourist boats that cruise there. This was little short of miraculous and a feat no adult would have accomplished without body armour or being contained in a barrel. His safe landing happened probably because, lacking the baggage of adult anticipatory fear, he surrendered to the situation and relaxed into his plunge. Fifty years later, he now describes a feeling of peace as he actually tumbled over the edge. He has no memory of his landing, although he well remembers the fear of being thrown along by the white water at the head of the Falls. I wonder what I could learn from him as I and my country stand trembling on the edge of our own plunge. Our currency has already gone ahead of us. It would appear that in such situations we have only two options: either to foresee the calamitous fall and set up defences to prevent us going over the edge, or, if this proves to be impossible, to surrender to the drop and prepare to resume our journey, bruised and battered, in a new place.

On a lighter note, you may be interested to learn that if you have ever had to bail out of a burning aircraft using a parachute, you may be eligible for membership of the exclusive *Caterpillar Club*. You can check out your credentials on the internet. One applicant was famously refused because his parachute had also caught fire, and he had been forced to make his descent from the stricken aircraft in free fall. He landed, most fortuitously, in a snow-drift. Perhaps there should be a special category of Unusually Unlucky Caterpillars for such as he. And perhaps we might also be reminded that just as there can be worse luck hidden inside bad luck, so too there can be unexpected blessings hidden inside apparently unmitigated disasters. The motto of the Caterpillar Club is: '*Life depends on a silken thread*'. Such is the wisdom of the chrysalis.

Most of us will be spared such dramatic demonstrations of the good luck – bad luck dynamic. The children's game of Snakes and Ladders is a more familiar example and one that gives me hope. We have no choice as to where the throw of the die, or the turn of events, will land us. It may be at the head of a snake or the bottom of a ladder. But on those occasions in life where we do indeed slide down the longest snake, losing all we have gained along our way so far, that same fall can bring us closer to the foot of the longest ladder. Opportunity and danger walk hand in hand in every crisis, so the Chinese wisdom assures us. When the snake has been of our own making it is harder to remain so phlegmatic. But consider this: if we are capable of making snakes, we are also capable of making ladders.

Opportunities, however, usually come in flat pack form. We get the raw materials delivered, but it's up to us what we make of them. It may be that humanity will go over the waterfall in the foreseeable future. If that happens, our question should not be: 'Whom shall we blame for this?' but rather 'How will we move forward, together, in this new phase of the river's flow? And given my own ineptitude with anything that comes out of a flat pack, I am quite convinced that this is going to be a communal project.

IN THE DARK

Do you wake up sometimes feeling very much in the dark, even if it's well after sunrise? Do you have days when things really look so gloomy that you can't see any way ahead? A bit like being out on the moors when the fog comes down, or driving through a long tunnel without being able to see any light at the end of it?

Such times might give us insight into how the caterpillar feels when it has become a chrysalis. It's dark in there, and nothing is remotely as it once was. All orientation has been lost. There are no waymarks to provide direction and indeed it feels as though there is nowhere to go. The ex-caterpillar has no idea of what will happen next. We too, in our present global and national situation have no idea what to do next. In the UK even our political leaders who brought us to the edge of this cliff have to admit that we are all now walking in the dark. Some would say we are *sleep*-walking into the dark. The future is always an unknown quantity, but in the past there have usually been models or patterns of how to navigate the waters. Now we are truly walking along a road that has not only not been walked before, but has not yet even been constructed.

What do we do in this darkness? In *Hidden Wings* we reflected on the fact that one obvious response to the outside darkness is to draw the curtains closed and shut it out. The general term for this reaction is 'denial'. It involves shutting ourselves down against the events we don't want to acknowledge in the outside

93

world, like a baby hiding under a blanket to protect himself from the thunderstorm, or his parents switching off the TV because they can no longer cope with the news it transmits. No one wants to look into the dark so we construct other, more manageable things to look at instead. We project our own patterns onto these curtains, and they offer welcome distraction from the big questions that are trying to gain our attention. What do some of these 'curtains' look like in practice? What kind of issues are commandeering our attention, while all the while the deep dark may be calling us to higher levels of consciousness, beyond our smaller preoccupations?

Some suggestions:

Comfort patterns of all the good things our consumer society places before us, inviting – even urging – us to buy things we neither want nor need, and to do so using 'credit' (which, until the bankers changed its name and with that its image, used to be known by its honest name: *debt*). The emperor Nero is famous for 'fiddling while Rome burned'. Are we also tempted to 'fiddle', with the trivia of consumerism, while the future of ourselves and our planet is in jeopardy?

Religious comfort (or control) patterns that we have probably grown up with, but, seen through more mature eyes, we may need to call into question. Our spiritual journey may also have moved into a dark tunnel, where the childhood certainties dissolve into the night. We may have shed the controlling strictures that promise eternal rewards in heaven for good behaviour on earth and increasingly resemble the voices of our parents and teachers. The patterns on our religious 'curtains' may be fading, and that may be no bad thing. The true mystery we are searching for may lie in the deeper darkness within and beyond us, both concealed and revealed by the stars.

Nationalist patterns that are far from fading. Indeed they

are becoming more and more evident. What do you make of the nationalist flags that are flying today? How do you feel about the kind of patriotism that is based on 'My country first!' and 'My country, right or wrong'? Let me put this thought to you. There is, as I see it, a big difference between nationalism and nationhood. Raw nationalism, such as we are experiencing now in some sectors of society, is in danger of becoming defensive, protectionist, and intolerant of other ways of being human on this planet. It builds fences where we desperately need bridges. Nationhood is very different. It cherishes the unique traditions and gifts of different national cultures and languages, recognising that each brings something very special to the human family, without generating antagonism in the process. Nationalism is a sign of *de*-volution, or regression from the evolutionary path. It has the potential to seduce us into the very worst to which humanity can sink, as history has revealed. Nationhood, at its best, is *e*-volutionary, helping us to grow more fully into the best we can be. A community of nations, working together, however haltingly, towards a better future, while each bringing their own treasure to the table is an excellent expression of this movement.

In this contrast of nationalism and nationhood, fences and bridges, turning in defensively or reaching out creatively, where do you feel your country locates itself in the present times?

There is something else in the darkness. Darkness is where things grow. Most good things grow in the dark, from bulbs to babies. Might it therefore not be true that humanity can grow in the dark? In fact the darkness we are living through in our times may be a very necessary ingredient of our growth. Spiritual energy dances in the dark, in ways we cannot begin to imagine. The same spirit invites us to join the dance, whether or not we know the steps or glimpse the signs of dawn. But to really look into this potentially life-giving darkness, we will need to open the curtains, look beyond our lesser concerns, shake ourselves free of the denial and gaze at the stars.

SILENCE IS NOT ALWAYS GOLDEN

Sometimes silence is leaden. Have you ever sent off an important letter or email and waited in vain for a response, wondering whether you have caused offence and may never hear what the recipient really felt about what you said?

Or have you ever given someone a gift that you really believed would please them, but received no acknowledgement, and been left feeling that something of yourself has been rejected?

Or have you ever tip-toed carefully through a family gathering or a dinner with friends, consciously avoiding mentioning any of a number of controversial or sensitive issues? This situation is what we commonly call 'an elephant in the room.' Everyone knows it is there, and that it is actually dominating our thoughts, but we tacitly agree not to mention it, in case it runs wild and wrecks the furniture.

Such discretion can sometimes be helpful for the sake of good relationships. Sometimes it can be harmful because it can leave crucially important issues un-discussed and unresolved. There are more elephants than usual in our living rooms at present. One thing about elephants is that they get bigger and more of a liability the longer we let them occupy our favourite armchairs, fearful of poking them into action. What could happen if we do name them and cause them to stir?

The silence of division is one of our current elephantine villains. Following very divisive votes in 2016 in the UK and the

US, roughly half the population found that their opinions were no longer welcome. Some pubs in England have even found it necessary to install a 'fine box' for anyone who mentions 'Brexit'. In the US there are citizens who cannot bring themselves to name names but refer to their duly elected president simply as '45'. In both countries there are people who won't speak to other family members 'on the other side'. Such painful divisions are not the result of normal political disagreement. They reflect very real distress and confusion about primal human issues like identity, loyalty, and a sense of belonging. They stem from the heart of much of what it means to be human and, like physical wounds, if they are not attended to they will become septic.

Simply ignoring these, and other deep social wounds, in the hope that they will go away, is also running counter to the very principle of democracy and is tantamount to suppressing opposition. In fact, of course, healthy democracy absolutely needs healthy opposition to keep calling the government of the day, or the decision of the hour, to account. Yet in the UK millions of people were told to 'suck it up' and stop being 'bad losers', as though the entire matter had been merely a game of cards or a football match. There were even voices accusing anyone who continued to oppose the UK's exit from the EU of treason and demanding that they should be silenced, while the governing party openly condemned opposition voices in parliament as 'saboteurs'. The heavily loaded words 'enemies of the people' have also raised their ugly heads on both sides of the Atlantic, with all the baggage of historic totalitarianism. History reminds us, all too painfully, that the silencing of opposition is a mark of fascism. These are ugly warnings indeed, and silence is a conspirator in this dangerous deal.

But how do you wake a sleeping elephant? How do you begin to break the silent tensions around these divisive issues? Not by brute force I suggest. I was taught something about this art in a most unexpected way by someone who, I knew, disagreed with me on some significant issues – so much so that I steered clear of him, for fear of getting into verbal conflict. Then one day, in a Quaker meeting of all places, he approached me and asked, in a friendly manner, how life was treating me. So I told him, but his courtesy and tolerant listening modified my response too, and I was able to share with him the very deep pain I was feeling and as I spoke, I could *see* him listening – it was visible in his eyes. The elephant I had been avoiding with him for many months had finally been named, but in a civilised manner that led both of us to a deeper level of trust and understanding. I am very grateful to him. It was an evolutionary moment.

Can we find ways of talking to each other, and, even more importantly, *listening* to each other, in a way that takes us beyond the painful divisions without shying away from the important issues that we absolutely must discuss if we are not to go like lemmings over the edge of disaster, informed only by dishonest journalism and toxic politics.

But sometimes actions speak louder than words, and the person we *are* is more eloquent than the words we speak or write. The greatest tragedy of the whole deeply damaging referendum campaign in the UK was the assassination of one of our finest politicians, Jo Cox – an idealist of absolute integrity, much loved by her constituents and a tireless campaigner for tolerance, peace, social justice and international cooperation. As he stabbed her to death, her murderer uttered the words 'Britain first'. Her life will continue to shine out on humanity's horizon as a beacon to new beginnings, where so many others have misled and deceived us. There is hardly anyone in the UK, of whatever persuasion, who, I believe, would disagree. In her life and in her tragic and premature death, she was, and is, a bridge that even now can lead us over troubled waters.

We can't all be a Jo Cox, but we can all choose, in our own life situations, to walk the way of integrity. Honesty, transparency, compassion and truth will not be handed down from above on a plate or by act of parliament. They must be worked out, and lived out, in our individual lives. We work them out, and live them out every time we have a meaningful conversation with someone with whom we disagree, every time we speak out if we hear a stranger in our land being abused or made to feel unwelcome, every time we make a stand when we can see injustice or bigotry in our own communities and our own country. But let's not lose sight of the fact that injustice begins in our own hearts, which is the only region where we can effect real and lasting change.

May we have the courage to speak when integrity demands it, the humility to be quiet when kindness requires it, and the wisdom to know the difference.

Audre Lorde, writer and civil rights activist, expresses it like this:

'The fact that we are here and that I speak these words is an attempt to break that silence and bridge some of those differences between us, for it is not difference which immobilises us, but silence. And there are so many silences to be broken.'

HIDDEN, HELPLESS, HOPELESS?

These three words express something of the feeling of being caught painfully between the No Longer and the Not Yet. Even more disturbing and immediate than the nostalgic desire to go back to an ill-remembered past, or the impetus to move quickly forward to an illusory future, is the painful impotence of the in-between-time:

I am invisible, curled up here in my cocoon
There is absolutely nothing I can do about the situation in which I find myself
There is not so much as a gleam of hope penetrating the darkness inside my shell

Invisibility can engulf you more rapidly, and with less benefit, than the Invisibility Cloak of a Harry Potter story. I never imagined that a western democracy could be so intolerant of dissent until 24 June 2016. Many US citizens might say the same about waking up on 9 November of the same year. These are dates we will never forget, because suddenly all the din and racket of squalid and destructive political campaigning fell silent like a ceasefire. Half of us, in both countries, woke to find that we were expected to bury our very real concerns and disappear into the shadows.

This wasn't just the material of journalism or cartoons. It

was personal. It was very painfully personal, to discover that citizenship of a country that prided itself on being the cradle of modern democracy counted for so little. Opposition was not wanted. Dissenters were an embarrassing nuisance to be dismissed and even in some cases ridiculed and vilified. The values I had thought we shared as a nation – values of openness, freedom of speech and diversity of opinion, internationalism, compassion for refugees, fair dealings, and peaceful co-operation with our neighbours were being eroded day on day, as more and more hate crime, more xenophobic rhetoric flooded our airwaves, hi-jacked our headlines and defiled our streets. It felt like waking up in a different country – one in which people from other countries suddenly no longer felt welcome, one in which I might not actually want to live myself.

Yet there was nothing at all that anyone felt able to do. The inefficacy of the official opposition was shameful, and yet the impossibility of personal opposition felt even worse. Now, as I think of the chrysalis, I can see that this kind of helplessness is the hallmark of the whole process. It is precisely in its utter helplessness that the caterpillar is being transformed by forces and energies far beyond its own control. Can I really believe that this could be true in our personal and national situations? To believe this is an act of faith. It calls me to live by a different story – the story of potential transformation. And by living by it, to make it real.

Helplessness is a very unpleasant experience. It can easily lead to hopelessness when all you want to do is curl up, close down, or emigrate. 'Hope' is easily talked about – a commodity we sometimes rather glibly offer each other when we don't know what else we can do. It can be just a religious platitude or an emotional analgesic. Or it can be a lifeline when we feel we are drowning, a lighthouse in the storm, a friend who is simply there at our side, no words needed.

A midwife friend surprised me one day when she told me about the 'transition phase' that occurs between the first and second stages of labour. After the agonising contractions of the first stage, she told me, the birthing mother is likely to express deep weariness, and want to give up on the whole enterprise. Yet this is the experience that immediately precedes the big push.

There are times when we do need to curl up and close down, exactly as the caterpillar does as it disintegrates into the chrysalis, or as a trauma patient might need to be helped towards recovery through a medically-induced coma. And there are times when the very opposite is needed. We need to wake up and be attentive as the energy of transformation takes its course. Sometimes we need a holiday. Sometimes we need to roll up our sleeves and be proactive. Sometimes we need to throw our energy into agitating for positive change, or into resisting negative movements. Sometimes we need to carry the flickering candle of hope for each other. Ancient wisdom promises that 'I will not crush the bruised reed or snuff out the flickering candle.' This may be a promise from eternity, but it is also an imperative to us in the here and now, as we take care of each other in the hazardous and terrifying darkness of the chrysalis.

A COSMOS IN
EVERY CHAOS

Yes, it would be very easy to despair, deep inside the darkness of the chrysalis, and even to question whether it really *is* a chrysalis and not a black hole. Carl Jung is the author of the wisdom of the title of this chapter: 'In all chaos there is a cosmos,' he asserts, 'in all disorder a secret order'. If this is true, then there really is hope that some new order is coming to be within the heart of our present global disorder. The truth of this is not just an optimistic statement by a renowned psychologist, but it is affirmed in every branch of human endeavour – in the physics and mathematics of chaos theory, in the pattern of life, death, disintegration and rebirth in the entire natural order from single-celled organisms to entire galaxies, in the wisdom of sacred scriptures and in our own personal experience of how new possibilities can often arise out of apparently negative situations.

Chaos theory might not be the first thing on your mind when you are debating the latest political twist down at the pub, but it could just possibly be the most important messenger to our world today. It tells us, on the one hand, what we already know very well – that every so often ordered systems break down into disorder, but, more significantly, that in the heart of the chaotic breakdown lies the incipient pattern of an emerging new beginning. This new pattern, which scientists tell us is initiated by the *strange attractor*, will be self-similar, in that it resembles the patterns it replaces, but is also radically new, taking us in a fresh direction. There is a recurring message in Christian scripture that a seed has to die and disintegrate so that the new life it contains can be released. This is pure chaos theory in ancient teaching.

A friend of mine, an Anglican priest, decided in her seventies that she wanted to learn to surf. While riding the ocean in Western Australia she found herself being sucked down by a large wave. Terrified she clung for dear life to her surfboard, fully believing this moment would be her last. She told me afterwards that instead of praying at that moment she could only think to herself 'What a stupid way to die!' Then the breakthrough came. The power of the sea forced the surfboard out of her grasp. Once freed of what she believed was her only hold on life, she had no choice but to surrender to her situation, at which point the waves brought her back safely to the surface.

There comes a point in our human endeavours at which we can do no more, and we are forced by circumstance to let go of our tenuous control. Then, and only then, can the strange attractor bring forth the new beginning. The caterpillar reaches the point of irreversible disintegration as it dissolves into the chrysalis state. And precisely in that chaotic breakdown of deconstruction lies the embryonic butterfly, still under construction, hidden away in the imaginal cells.

What new patterns of evolving humanity might potentially be emerging out of the chaotic breakdown of our present situations?

The seed of the new dawn germinates in the deepest dark of the night. To trust this wisdom, we may have to go deeper than our conventional religious platitudes, to touch the bedrock of human experience all through the ages, that life always yields to death and death always yields new life.

Nor is it just about what happens in the dark. It's about what can happen in empty space – and perhaps *only* in empty space. Ancient wisdom speaks of creation *ex nihilo* – out of nothing, out of emptiness, and the many archetypal stories of virginal birth are also reflections of the deep intuition that emptiness holds potential that is often denied to fullness.

The chrysalis is in some respects an empty space – empty, at least, of meaning, where neither the caterpillar-meaning nor the butterfly-meaning has form or shape – yet something profoundly life-giving is happening in that inchoate space. I was vividly reminded of the potency of emptiness one June evening in the French town of Chartres. It was the twilight hour, and the cathedral of Chartres would normally have closed at seven o'clock in the evening. As I walked past with a friend, however, we heard the faint sound of organ music emanating from the magnificent building.

Attracted by the sound, on closer investigation we discovered a small door that was still open. The great cathedral was almost empty – just a handful of people who, like ourselves, had been drawn in by the haunting music. The fading light filtered through the stained glass windows, bathing the cathedral in a mystical sheen, and the music poured itself freely into every nook and crevice of the vast edifice, like a mighty river that has at last found its true, unimpeded course. The magic of the hour only revealed itself in the semi-darkness and the almost-emptiness.

Now, as I reflect back on the sacred hour I spent in that sacred space, I can almost see the action of the strange attractor, drawing us in to the heart of the holy, there to reveal a very different experience of a world-renowned place – indeed a World Heritage Site – that we could never have expected or imagined, and so unlike the daylight visitor experience. And beneath the rows of pews (except on Fridays when it is revealed) lies the famous Chartres labyrinth, which is another invitation to walk the twisting pathways of our experience towards the deep and holy centre where new possibilities may reveal themselves. The memory of that June evening is imprinted in my heart. It gives me hope that transformative power can also be at work in my own, and our world's, darkness and emptiness. Twilight can be the cusp of a new dawn. Emptiness can be brimming with new life.

One more matter before we leave the dark recesses of breakdown. If you are familiar with *Hidden Wings*, you may remember the cautionary tale of Cousin Moth, who is a night flyer and tends to be attracted to any kind of light, mistaking it for a light by which to navigate. As a result, poor Moth frequently comes to a sticky end by flying into hot light bulbs, candle flames or bonfires, none of which are healthy destinations. Taking this phenomenon as a metaphor, there is a very stark warning for us here. Human beings, among all earth's creatures, are quite possibly among the most gullible. In the UK there were very many people in 2016 who believed an impossible promise just because it was emblazoned on the side of a campaign bus. To put our trust in such blatant propaganda is to risk flying straight into the bonfire. However, it is by no means always so obvious that we are being deceived by a bright light that we mistake for the sun or moon, but actually turns out to be something that will destroy us.

Let us be very discerning about the lights we trust to guide us, especially in these times in which the lines between truth and falsehood have been deliberately blurred. To be deceived is excusable. To be a deceiver is not.

CONVERSATION STARTERS ...

 PERSONAL IMPLICATIONS

When have you experienced a drop over the waterfall? How did the river run on after the fall?

When has the Chinese wisdom proved trustworthy in your own life, that crisis brings danger, but also opportunity? Our world is in the grip of multiple crises, most of them the result of human mismanagement or deliberate abuse. The dangers are obvious. Where do you see the opportunities?

When have you felt invisible, silenced, powerless, and even hopeless? What, or who, helped you to move on? Does anyone close to you need you to carry the hope for them right now?

Have you ever been seduced into walking a path that you later found to be destructive or harmful, because you were misled by false information?

 NATIONAL AND GLOBAL IMPLICATIONS

Do you recognise any of the patterns we project onto the curtains we draw to screen out the darkness? To what extent, for example, do you think religious threats and promises are 'curtain patterns' constructed by human beings to keep other human beings under control?

What does the word 'patriotism' mean to you? How would you view the difference between nationalism and nationhood?

Are there any elephants in your living room, or your family's living rooms, or in your local pub or coffee shop or anywhere else where two or more are gathered? Are you able to name them, and thereby rob them of their power?

Which tendencies in your own life and the life of your nation do you see as *evolutionary*? Which do you see as *devolutionary*. What might you do yourself to nourish all that is helping us to grow and *evolve* spiritually? What could you do to reduce the effects of anything that is causing us to regress and *devolve* spiritually?

 SPIRITUAL IMPLICATIONS

Can you tell the difference between the silence of denial and the silence of contemplation? How willing are you to break the former, and how comfortable are you in practising the latter? What spiritual practices might help you to live more contemplatively?

What does your religious/spiritual tradition teach about the meaning of breakdown as the gateway to breakthrough? How does it guide you through the times of darkness and the death of your hopes and dreams? Have you found its promise of new life emerging from apparent death to be true?

What does your religious/spiritual tradition suggest about where our first loyalty should lie: to our country or to the greater good of humanity as a whole? How does your own heart answer this question?

The opening quotation for this section reminds us that part of us has to die if we are to transform and part of us will die if we don't. How does this observation strike you when reflecting on the spiritual future of humankind?

PART 4
THE WAITING ROOM

'Do not be daunted by the enormity of the world's grief. Do justly, now. Love mercy, now. Walk humbly, now. You are not obligated to complete the work, but neither are you free to abandon it.'

(Interpretive translation of Talmudic text)

ANYTHING CAN HAPPEN IN THE WOODS

At this point the butterfly, still in formation, is hanging apparently helplessly inside the chrysalis. She is slowly becoming who she is. Such an undertaking takes *time*, and time is at a premium in our frenzied age. Our western societies just don't *do* time. Delayed gratification isn't popular. We want it all, and we want it *now*, and this impatient insistence is reflected everywhere back to us along our high streets, from fast food to guaranteed instant results.

It takes time to get used to this dark, empty, disconnected space. Dark for lack of any waymarks, any maps, any light at the end of the tunnel. Empty of all the meanings that previously guided our life. Empty it feels, even, of meaning itself, for what meaning can there be in this helpless hanging, this waiting for something that may not even be real or possible. Disconnected from the links that once held us together, bereft of the old relationships, cut off from the old communions and traditions. This is the waiting room, but it feels like a tomb.

These feelings remind me of the film *Into the Woods*, a playful exploration of what happens when the characters from familiar fairy tales get mixed up 'in the woods', all striving to live out their own familiar story, all striving to get their own wishes, as their stories prescribe, and then living with the consequences of those wishes. But of course, as the characters pursue what they believe to be their own story they clash with others who are pursuing *theirs*. In summary, as the script says 'These woods are dangerous … Anything can happen in the woods'. We can lose all sense of who we are and how we are supposed to proceed in these radically changed circumstances. A particularly ludicrous moment, but a moment loaded with meaning for us today, is when the Baker's Wife tries to press the STOP button in her panicked realisation:

> *'This is ridiculous. What am I doing here? I'm in the wrong story.'*

Here in the darkness of the chrysalis there is time and space to ponder the story. But in order to ponder the deeper story, the lesser stories will first have a crisis of their own. Like the characters in the film, each of our stories, both personal and national, will try to work itself out by the only rules it knows – the rules we ourselves have written, in our efforts to make sense of ourselves. The caterpillar story was all worked out. It was about eating until you burst and then expanding into a bigger container. It was about protecting yourself against a hostile environment, and, if necessary, becoming hostile yourself to get the other guy before he gets you. It was most certainly not about butterflies, because butterflies haven't been invented yet. They fly far beyond caterpillar imagination.

So it isn't hard to imagine the cells here in the chrysalis, surveying in dismay the mayhem of dissolution all around them, protesting 'What am I doing here? I'm in the wrong story.' Only the imaginal cells, who already hold the evolving butterfly, might intuit a bigger story, glimpse a longer vision.

In a blog post Denise Simone explains it like this:

'Our stories are nothing more than false interpretations of our past experience.'

Personally I would want to say *incomplete*, rather than *false* interpretations, but otherwise this is a good way of understanding how, as she goes on to say:

'Our stories keep us stuck and confined in a cocoon... We believe that what we currently see is the only possibility that exists.'

We can't by-pass this painful experience of being in the waiting room, where we don't know what we are waiting for or whether, indeed, there is anything at all to wait for. This is the only way to move from our small stories towards the bigger story. It expresses a lot of what we are going through in our present national and global crises. Everything seems to be going crazy. We don't know what we are doing here. We have lost the plot. We are in the wrong story.

The truth is a little more reassuring. We haven't lost the plot. The plot is just a lot bigger than we ever imagined, and we are moving into another chapter of it. We are still trying to live with an interpretation of our past experience that is no longer satisfactory – not because it is completely false, but because it is necessarily incomplete. The emergence of the butterfly can never fit the interpretation of life in a caterpillar narrative. The emergence of a fuller, truer, more complete version of humanity can never fit into the interpretation of life in our present narrative. This doesn't invalidate our present narrative, but it does ask of us that we re-consider it critically and discard those parts of it that no longer fit – parts like imperialism, nationalism, sectarianism, protectionism, isolationism, triumphalism. Yes, 'ism' seems to be rather an overworked suffix in the old narrative, doesn't it?

The gift of the waiting room is *time* to do this re-considering, and *space* to expand into the larger narrative that beckons us forward – to let work begin on the next edition of Project Humanity.

Anything can happen in the woods. And, for sure, we are not yet out of the woods.

SEEING WHAT'S NOT THERE YET

There's an inspirational BBC TV show called *DIY SOS*. Its ethos is to help people who have, for various serious personal reasons, come unstuck with well-intentioned DIY projects. The team achieves a remarkable makeover by employing a very small group of professionals to manage the project and motivating a much larger army of local volunteers, who just want to help a family in trouble.

One of the most inspirational episodes ended with this little story:

'Once upon a time there was a little girl who lived in a rundown old caravan next to a pile of rubble. Her father used to tell her: "One day that pile of rubble will become a wonderful home". Years passed and the dream seemed to be out of reach. The little girl's mum died, and her dad became seriously ill. Then one day an army came over the hill and turned that pile of rubble into a beautiful new home. And the magic of it was that this army didn't come from far away – but from the little girl's own village, and the nearby villages.'

To watch, on the programme, the joy on that little girl's – and her father's – face, as they were shown the transformed pile of rubble, as she explored what was now nothing less to her than a palace fit for a princess, restored my faith in the possibility of human transformation.

And like all significant transformations, it emerged out of a chaotic breakdown. The child's father had begun the project of building a family home, but his dream and his intention had been destroyed, first by traumatic bereavement and then by life-threatening illness. It had seemed that he and his little daughter would have to live in the rundown caravan for ever, cramped, cold and desolate.

But as we have seen again and again, adversity and opposition can kill the dreamer, but they can never kill the dream. In this case the dream that had apparently died at the hand of tragic loss and serious sickness, was resurrected by the care, compassion and commitment of fifty or so good neighbours and local tradespeople who transformed a pile of rubble into a home. They couldn't bring back the lost loved one. They couldn't cure the illness. But they could – and they did – give a little girl and her father a new beginning – warmth, comfort and a degree of real security against a still very uncertain future.

When the father publicly thanked all those who had contributed to this transformation, he made this comment: 'The house is amazing, and I thank you all so much. But even if there had been no house, just to see so many people gathered here to show that they care about us, means everything, and it gives me a reason to get up in the morning.'

This is what imagination can mean in our ordinary human lives. Perhaps each of us secretly dreams of fairy castles arising out of the rubble of our experience, but evolutionary imagination asks of us: 'What if life-changing transformation could be made possible for someone in the community, how could we come together to make it happen?'

There are as many ways of doing this as there are people

desperately in need of it. Most of us don't have the resources to build new homes, but sometimes it takes no more than a smile, a friendly conversation, an open door and a cup of tea to begin to change a life. Every one of us has a unique gift, called the Power of One. When many Ones come together, motivated by love and compassion, then the Power of Many can be released. The Power of Many is always more than the sum of all the Ones. The magic's in the maths.

In the darkness of the chrysalis, in the frustration of the cramped and windowless waiting room, it's easy to lose hope. But perhaps it is only in the profound darkness of not knowing, not understanding, not being able to move things on as we might wish, that we see what is not yet there, just as it is only in the deep darkness of the night, through the un-curtained, unprotected windows of the heart, that we see the stars.

What can we learn for our own times from this story of transformation?

Doesn't it tell us that our dreams really can become reality even though we can't yet imagine what that reality might look like or how it could be implemented? We dream of a transformed and matured humanity, living by the values we all cherish in our hearts, but rarely see embodied in our own lives or in the political life of our nations. What kind of army needs to come over the hill to make that a reality? I think we will find the answer is an army of people like us, all holding the Power of One, and working together to manifest the Power of All.

But this power isn't the oppressive kind of power that habitually rules our world. It is the creative, enabling power of love. This is the power that motivates ordinary folk to volunteer their services to make the dreams of a suffering neighbour become a reality. It is also the power that inspires people to produce programmes like *DIY SOS*. And it is the power that moves us so deeply when we hear these stories of human pain relieved and transformed, 'so that others might live'. It is quite simply the power of love, and all our spiritual traditions affirm that the power of love overcomes everything.

All these stories are truly heart-warming. Maybe this is exactly what is needed. Just as eggs only hatch when the mother bird incubates them by keeping them warm, so too our human hearts will only give birth to a new spiritual generation of humanity when they are warmed up. It would appear that at present human hearts, at least in our national and international affairs, are pretty cold. Whatever is heart-warming is surely key to our spiritual evolution. The invitation, therefore, is to nourish ourselves and each other with what warms us and makes us more human. Time, perhaps, to look at our spiritual diet, as we cherish the new possibility that is growing in our chrysalis time and space.

NOURISHING
TOMORROW

New beginnings don't grow on their own. Anyone who has experienced human pregnancy, either personally or by association, knows very well that the pregnant mother has to watch her diet. There are basically two rules:

Nourish the life that is coming.
Don't poison it.

Why would it be any different as we contemplate bringing to birth a new chapter of the whole human story? In Caterpillar World the imaginal cells literally carry the butterfly inside them. In Human World, the pregnant woman literally carries the next generation inside her. In Tomorrow's World each of us carries the possibility of our future inside ourselves. This future, quietly or sometimes turbulently (unborn babies can give you quite a kick!) asks to be cherished and nurtured. How we respond to its presence within us, while it is still unborn, will make or break the future towards which we are moving.

It has been a recurring theme of this book and of *Hidden Wings*, that each of us has a share of the responsibility for the kind of world we are co-creating. It is all too easy, and greatly encouraged by the general complacency of our western societies, to assume that the future will unfold as it will, and that we can do little if anything, to shape it. We leave it all to our politicians, or others who take on the power of leadership, and we have seen, especially recently, what a risky position that is. The imaginal cells don't take this risk. They know they hold the future, and they go through all the initial opposition from 'the system' for as long as it takes, until at last the pendulum swings away from the desperate clinging to the past, and towards the free flight of the future.

If each of us has a role to play, that role begins *in utero*, as it were, while the future is still very much in formation, as it is now in our times. So it matters how we will nourish that future, and it matters that we don't poison it. What might nourish our collective future, and the future of our planet, and what might poison it?

Traditional wisdom reminds us that 'Two men gaze through prison bars; the one sees mud, the other stars.' Most human situations are like that. It's very possible to see plenty of mud through the bars of our narrow worldview, and then to complain about what we see, and despair of anything ever improving. It only takes a slight adjustment of focus to see the stars instead. One way to nourish tomorrow is to take time to reflect over each passing day, and very intentionally to notice the stars that have lifted our hearts – the moments of gratitude, of wonder, of compassion, for example. When this becomes a habit, gradually the mud ceases to dominate our minds and the stars begin to illumine the darkness, as only stars can.

What we nourish will grow. What we starve will shrink. Take a look back over your day, your week, your year. Which aspects of that period were expanding and warming your heart and the hearts of those around you? Were there any aspects of the period that were sowing seeds of discontent or discord in you and in others? Where do you feel your energy and attention was mainly focused? Getting in touch with the patterns of your own energy flows in this way can be the beginning of understanding how you personally can nourish the future and avoid poisoning it with negativity.

But of course this doesn't mean smiling – Pollyanna-style – at whatever happens. When we meet negative situations there are two options. We can either let them go and refuse to give them our attention, which in turn will take power away from them, as one might withdraw attention from a toddler during a tantrum – or we can actively work against them. Some situations are so serious that they require real, and even passionate, resistance and opposition.

Perhaps the most reliable guidance comes from the tried and tested wisdom of the Serenity Prayer:

'May we have the serenity to accept what we cannot change, the courage to change what can, and must, be changed, and the wisdom to know the difference.'

When we find ourselves in a situation that we neither chose nor desired, learning to see what we can and cannot change is essential, and then, having discerned the difference, to find the courage to make what changes we can. How does this logic work out for you now, in your present circumstances?

POT-BOUND

I don't have green fingers. I can kill most things in pots. This is not a characteristic of which I am proud. However, my failure on one occasion did teach me something that was about more than plants. After about three months following its purchase from a local garden centre, a plant died on me. I wanted to replace it, but I also wanted to know what I had done wrong to it, to cause its demise, so I went back to the garden centre to ask for their advice.

I was told, very kindly, that my plant had been 're-potted at the wrong time.' It was confession time again as I had to admit that I hadn't re-potted it at all. The response to this was that they themselves must have re-potted it, and they offered to replace it. This hadn't been my intention, but I took the opportunity to ask them about the rules of re-potting, so that I might be able to avoid future fatalities.

The wisdom they passed on involved these basic rules:

Plants grow out of their pots and need to be transferred to bigger pots, otherwise the roots will not have space to expand, and the plant will eventually die

The re-potting is best done at the beginning of a season of growth

The plant should be moved from its too-small pot to the next size up, and not simply flung out into an open field, with no boundaries to contain its growth.

The process should be repeated as long as the plant keeps growing out of its container.

This gem of horticultural wisdom transfers very aptly to the process of our spiritual growth. Very many people, it seems to me, are spiritually 'pot-bound' in our times. Those who have grown up inside the framework of organised religion frequently get stuck in a Sunday school theology. They have been taught the rules. They keep the rules. They confess their sins when they break the rules. And that's it. In some traditions any questioning of the received teaching is actively discouraged. Other people have leapt out of the pot, or have never been in it, and find themselves in the open field, with no framework at all.

What can we learn from all this? Two things spring to mind immediately for me.

First, we are, as a human family on this planet, precisely at the beginning of a whole new season of growth. Something is stirring deeply in the core of humanity. It is making waves, some of them dangerous, but it is like the stirring of an unborn child. Something's going on, and it is becoming impossible, even for those least interested in world affairs, to ignore these winds of change. The garden centre would say this is the time we are going to need a bigger pot. The containers that have held our understanding of ourselves and our place in the cosmos are too small. Religion is too small to contain our sense of the sacred. Nation states are too small to contain the global spirit of who we are.

Second, we should beware of leaping out of the pot completely, but allow ourselves to grow more gently into the future, making wise choices as we go. It's easy to assume that we would grow better if we abandon all religious practice, and yet, flawed though they may be, the religious structures that have become so constricting are also the structures that gave us the contained but protected place to do our early growing. Perhaps it is time to allow 'religion' to grow into a greater fullness of non-sectarian spirituality.

It's clear to see that our political and social systems are dysfunctional and it's tempting to abandon them completely. We are disillusioned with democracy, especially as it has recently delivered some dangerously world-changing outcomes, and yet democracy, flawed though it is, remains the best shot we have had so far at governing ourselves with a degree of consensus. Perhaps it is time to allow our national democracies to evolve into a greater fullness of a supra-national awareness, placing the earth and all her inhabitants before national self-interest.

The one thing that is certain is that if we don't find a bigger pot we will shrivel and die.

TIME FOR GATHERING

At this point in the cycle of metamorphosis the various 'parts' of the coming butterfly have been growing quietly inside the imaginal cells, but a new creation doesn't come into being until the cells of which it is composed gather together to make more and more complex structures. This is how we all evolve from our first single-cell beginning to our mature complexity. It is also the evolutionary pattern identified by Teilhard de Chardin, through attraction to connection to complexity and ultimately towards heightened consciousness. In this process we now reach the challenge of *connection*.

No less than in the world of the butterflies, our own spiritual evolution requires that each of us brings to the process our own unique contribution, allowing our individual 'self' to be taken up into a greater whole. And so the time arrives, in our spiritual growth into a fully human family, when we must grow beyond the dependency of childhood, beyond the independence of adulthood, towards the *inter-dependency* of full maturity. The butterfly begins in the dependency of the caterpillar world, where it can be held back and suppressed by the controlling immune system, to the independence of the imaginal cell that knows it holds the future but is not quite there yet, to the inter-dependency of a complex new multi-celled organism at which point it has transformed completely from the greedy grub of the forest to the flying flower of the skies.

It all sounds so easy, so obvious, and, in the case of the butterfly story, so inevitable. Our own progression from infant dependency to adult independence is also obvious if not always so easy. It becomes much more challenging, however, when the time arrives to move beyond independence to inter-dependence, and in that crucial next step we are still very much beginners.

Unfortunately 'independence' and autonomy' have acquired almost mystical significance in the western world, and are certainly viewed as goals to be aspired to in their own right. This can completely block the way forward to the 'more' of *inter*-dependence. It is wisely said that 'the good can be the enemy of the better'. Independence is certainly a state to be desired, as our children, for example, grow up and beyond their total need of us. For an adult the state of dependency is usually seen as a diminishment. But is this really so? I am reminded of the fictional character Sebastian Flyte in Evelyn Waugh's *Brideshead Revisited*. Sebastian is a very needy individual who has never quite achieved freedom from infantile dependency on others or learned to cope adequately with the demands of adult life. One could say he 'fails to thrive', and, for all intents and purposes goes rapidly downhill, becoming increasingly dependent on alcohol, and worse. Eventually, on his slide down the slippery slope, he finds another aimless wanderer, Kurt, who has no hesitation in exploiting his friend's wealth and good nature. Kurt is the kind of person every parent would warn their child against, but Sebastian takes upon himself the care of Kurt, and discovers, in the process, something of the great gift of inter-dependency. He expresses it like this:

'You know,' he said, 'it's rather a pleasant change when all your life you've had people looking after you, to have someone to look after yourself.'

Sebastian, 'the loser' has taken that great leap towards spiritual maturity in realising that we only really have meaning in relationship, and inter-dependent relationship involves surrendering something of one's untouchable autonomy. Sometimes human beings evolve most readily when we are de-throned from our heights of independence by the moral imperative to respond to another's need. Sometimes those who most truly understand inter-dependence are people who have experienced the most grievous loss and discovered the necessary mutual inter-connections among those who, for all kinds of reasons, have moved, or been pushed, to the margins of society.

The Chinese proverb tells us that 'if you save a life you are responsible for that life.' It sounds like a tough, and questionable, deal, but it makes a certain kind of sense in a climate of inter-dependence. Once we have recognised our kinship with each other, then we become responsible for each other's wellbeing. We can no longer live by the 'Me First' or 'My Country First' philosophy. This simple truth lies at the heart of all true spiritual traditions. Tragically, in our national and international relationships at the present time, the movement seems to be seriously regressive.

A lot is going on in the waiting room, even though it seems to be so motionless. We need patience to live in the waiting room and allow the new thing to come to be. But the emergence of new beginnings depends on an energy greater than our own. Whatever is happening there in the chrysalis is out of our control. We are way out of our familiar territory here. We are carrying what is not yet there, and all that we can do is nourish it, avoid poisoning it, and be willing to let go of the small ego-self we thought we were in order to become our true selves and embrace the challenge of co-creating a reality much greater than the sum of all our individual parts.

There is everything to learn in the waiting room, and we are proving to be rather slow and obstinate students of the new consciousness that is striving to emerge. Perhaps it's time for a reality check.

CONVERSATION STARTERS...

 PERSONAL IMPLICATIONS

In today's chaotically changing world, can you identify with the cry of 'I'm in the wrong story?' Which parts of your 'old story' do you think you need to let go, because they are no longer helpful or relevant?

How healthy is your imagination? Can you imagine possibilities you can't yet see? In the story of the DIY makeover the realisation of the dream is brought about by simple human compassion and co-operation. What can this teach us about the way forward, in realising our deepest dreams for the future of humanity?

 NATIONAL AND GLOBAL IMPLICATIONS

What 'story' do you think your own country is trying to live by at present? Is it in conflict with the stories of other nations? Is it perhaps time to let it grow into a bigger story?

How can national government grow into a vision that transcends national boundaries and self-interest? Could you play any part in achieving this at a local, national or international level?

When you consider the state of the world today and the state of your own country, what things warm your heart, and what is leaving you cold (or even provoking you to white-hot rage)? How can you nourish what is truly life-affirming for all creation and let go of, or actively work against what is life-diminishing or working against the flow of spiritual evolution?

No one wants to be 'dependent'. Everyone hopes to be 'independent'. How do you feel about the higher call, to become 'inter-dependent'? What would this mean for your own nation and society?

 SPIRITUAL IMPLICATIONS

What does your religious/spiritual tradition teach about the 'waiting time', the space between what has been left behind and what has not yet been arrived at?

Sacred scripture speaks of how we are carrying our own future inside us. Does your religious/spiritual practice nourish this hidden future? How can we co-operate by giving it positive and creative attention and energy? How can we avoid poisoning it with negative energy, hatred, prejudice or violent and divisive thoughts, words or actions?

Are we becoming spiritually 'potbound' in our smaller stories? Can the horticultural practice of re-potting help us to grow again?

Is our spiritual vision being limited and retarded by traditional 'religion'?

PART 5
THE DREAM
TAKES FLIGHT

*'At first dreams seem impossible,
then improbable, then inevitable'*

Christopher Reeve

ON THE CUSP OF A NEW BEGINNING

This journey may have left you feeling that it's a great idea to grow into a transformed humanity, but is it a realistic aspiration? A number of practical approaches have been suggested, but does the future still seem as impossible a hope as the future butterfly would seem to the caterpillar?

The first hint of the colours of the coming butterfly begin to show faintly through the wall of the chrysalis. The final stage of birthing is beginning, and the future will emerge from its womb in its own time and its own way. The dream is hatching. Take a moment to watch the emergence of a butterfly – there are lots of examples on YouTube.

All through the caterpillar stage the dream seemed impossible. If a caterpillar could watch a film of its own future it would shake its head and keep on munching. This creature about to emerge from the chrysalis which it has now outgrown can surely have nothing to do with caterpillars, it might say. The whole thing stretches credibility beyond all reasonable limits.

In the chrysalis there is a sense of something new coming to be. And yet the chrysalis time is so terrible, the meltdown so absolute, that the dream that quivers in the imaginal cells still seems highly improbable. So too, the possibility of a more highly evolved humanity still seems improbable, to say the least, while we struggle with all the dissolution of our own chrysalis time – just as the black butterfly seemed like an improbable fantasy to Ali's friends as they sat at her bedside and accompanied her through the dissolution of her final illness.

And then the moment of emergence. The newly metamorphosed butterfly flutters on the cusp of a future it could never have imagined, and now, at last, the dream has become inevitable.

And our human dreaming? How might *our* impossible dream take flight, the dream of a world transformed? How might it show its improbable colours through the skin of the chrysalis? How might it engage in the inevitability of its coming-to-birth?

When the butterfly is fully formed within the chrysalis its next challenge is to find its way out. This isn't easy. There are stories told about people who watched a butterfly struggling to disentangle itself from the fibres of the cocoon, and tried to cut it free. As a result of this well-meaning intervention the butterfly invariably died – not because it was harmed by the scissors, but because a butterfly needs the birth struggle in order to initiate the circulation to its wings. If this doesn't happen, it can't fly, and therefore it can't live.

It is probably true to say that no living creature comes to birth on this planet without a birth struggle of some kind. This is certainly true for our own species. Anyone who has given birth, or been present at a birth, knows just how hard it can be for the mother to enable that tiny baby to make his or her appearance. The process is not called 'labour' for nothing.

It should not surprise us, therefore, that the process of birthing a new future for humanity on this planet will also involve a struggle. It seems to be a necessary component of all birthing that the one giving birth has to face pain and difficulty.

What signs do we see in our world today of this necessary struggle to become the best we can be? Some suggestions:

- The struggle taking place among all people of good will (the vast majority of human beings) against the shadow side of humanity revealing itself in outbreaks of brutality, abuse and acts of terrorism.

- The struggle to discern how best to govern ourselves, when the limitations of our current practice of party-dominated democracy, among an uninformed, or deliberately mis-informed electorate, are becoming painfully clear.

- The struggle between truth and falsehood, in a world in which integrity has largely been sacrificed to political expediency and blatant propaganda.

- The struggle to resist slipping into chronic cynicism in a world in which neither the voices of political leaders and opinion-shapers, nor the intentions and motivations of either commercial organisations or official institutions can be trusted.

- The struggle to discover what it really means to be a 'person of faith', and to live by that faith, when the traditional religious systems are losing credibility.

- The struggle to keep on believing that we can become a better version of ourselves, and to live towards that destiny, rather than succumbing to a fatalistic and unhappy acceptance of 'the way things are'.

- In the language of spiritual discernment, the struggle between the creative and the destructive spirits or energies flowing through our world and ourselves. The creative spirit, or the Holy Spirit, reveals itself through truth, compassion, gentleness, co-operation, trust and trustworthiness, and authentic hope. The destructive spirit reveals itself in fake news, alternative facts, inflammatory rhetoric, words and acts of hatred, negativity, unwarranted confrontation, attitudes of exclusion, the tendency to demonise those who think, live, speak or believe differently. These spirits, both the creative and the destructive, flow through, around and among us all. It is our choice and responsibility to nourish the creative spirit and withdraw our attention from, or work against the destructive spirit.

The birth process begins when the time is right. The maternal body knows when the foetus is ready to emerge. The chrysalis knows when the butterfly is ready to emerge. How do *we* know when it is time for a new and more fully human version of humanity, a heightened level of human consciousness, to emerge? An answer to this might be to observe the signs of the times. Prior to birthing there is usually a state of increasing unease, discomfort and turbulence. Something is afoot! There is pain. There is tension. There is a sense that the old order will have to be torn apart for the new to emerge. There can even be a desire to hold on, desperately, to the old order, for fear of what the new order might demand of us – a kind of misplaced nostalgia for how things used to be 'in the good old days', which, of course, were not so 'good' at all.

Do you notice any of these 'signs of the times' in our own day? Any turbulence and unease? Any discomfort with the way things are and yet a fear of any change? Any desire to artificially re-create 'the good old days'? Any pain and tension both personal and in the public domain?

When we look back in history we see how periods of

significant change (that Karen Armstrong calls 'axial ages') are usually preceded by the turbulence of radical change and a chaotic breakdown of the old order.

Are we living through an 'axial age' in our own times, when humanity is changing so rapidly and so profoundly that future historians and anthropologists will see this century as a watershed in human consciousness development?

If we are really in the midst of a spiritual birthing process, we should also remember that a baby who stays too long in the mother's womb will die. Once a new being is conceived, it must come to birth or die. Once a new version of humanity is conceived, it must come to birth, or die. If we persist in delaying or resisting the birth struggle, we will, in effect be aborting our own future.

UNANCHORED

Fear flies low and pulls us down, undermines us. Dreams fly high and call our hearts to rise. Everyday life hovers somewhere between the two. All kinds of circumstances determine whether at any given time our spirits are sinking or rising. In recent times, and during the writing of this book and its companion *Hidden Wings*, the direction for many of us, especially in the UK, has been down. The suction of fear, despair, anger and distrust has sometimes felt overwhelming. We are feeling adrift from ourselves and our nation and maybe also from our religious tradition, unanchored from what has hitherto held us where we felt we needed to be.

For me the image that best captures this response to what is happening in our nation, our society, our world today is a memory of snorkelling off a small boat on the west coast of Australia, and finding myself caught in a rip current. The drift away from the boat was initially almost imperceptible. My own drift away from the boat of my earlier life had also been happening, in quite important and healthy ways, over many years – the 'boat' being my former affiliation to particular branches of institutional religion, and my fairly unquestioning acceptance of my national identity and many rather complacent assumptions that went with it. The drift was taking me into wider, deeper oceans. It was part of a process of spiritual and emotional maturation.

Then came the rip current.

Suddenly, and frighteningly, I realised I was being pulled a long way from the boat. The ocean was churning. The politics were, and still are, toxic. Many of the politicians, not just in my own country, were behaving like playground bullies, with no regard at all for the good of the community, willing to alienate our nation's friends and neighbours, to flirt instead with dubious regimes for the sake of trade deals, and even to jeopardise the ideals of universal human rights and the future of the planet, for their own ego-centred purposes. My faith in my own country, in its essential tolerance and stability, my faith in its leaders, and even my faith in democracy itself were disappearing over a receding horizon.

Religious uncoupling was exacerbated by the manifest immorality of those who monopolised the 'moral high ground' yet stood in judgement over the rest of us, and also by the brutality that we could see, every day, walking hand in hand with religious fundamentalism. How, we had to ask, could the Christian tradition have drifted so far from the Man from Galilee, or our liberal democracy have strayed so far from its roots in reason, compassion and justice? Similar questions were clearly being asked by people of other faith traditions and in other countries. Was the entire world becoming unanchored?

When I hit the rip current in Australia I tried to swim, vigorously but in vain, against the tidal force, but also doing what I had been taught to do, raising my hand as a call for help, and the boat quickly came to rescue me. For quite some time I think I was trying to use the same method in the political rip current that the UK had voted itself into and a flurry of reckless leadership had precipitated. It took me a long time to realise that this was futile, and in any case, did I really want ever to return to that boat?

Those who know about rip currents, of course, advise a very different technique: swimming against the current will get you nowhere, and will wear you out. Instead you should strike a sideways course, to slip out of the rip stream and into steadier waters, and then discern your new course from this steady state, where a calmer, more reasoned approach to the turmoil might emerge.

This strikes me as sound guidance for handling the upheaval in our world today. Our immediate instinct might well be to struggle against the rip current, and, as we have already discovered, this will leave us exhausted and still thoroughly embroiled in the chaos. What does it mean, in practice, to strike a personal course out of the worst of the turbulence and find a steadier place to stand, from which to decide the next steps? Fighting is futile. Finding a place to be still and to reflect is essential and those next steps will almost certainly not lead back to the starting point, but will challenge us to find the most life-giving way to move on from the new point, however unwanted, to which the storm has brought us.

For the new-born child, just as for the newly emerged butterfly, there is no way back to the womb, the chrysalis, the boat. The first thing that happens to the new-born child, after she has been squeezed painfully out of the only home she ever had, is that the friendly midwife comes along with the sharp scissors and severs the umbilical cord, thus cutting off the baby's food supply. Not the most auspicious beginning to a life on earth. If the baby could articulate her feelings at this point it would surely feel like *deprivation*. She has been forcibly separated from her only source of nourishment. In fact, of course, it is *liberation*. She is now free to discover a wholly different kind of life, free to find all kinds of much more interesting meals than the placental food supply, free to explore a world so much more thrilling than the confines of the womb, free, in fact, to live.

Our newly-emerging butterfly also hangs by an 'umbilical cord' – the strong but slender thread by which it is attached to the branch that has supported it all through the dark chrysalis time. Now that connection will be broken. It reminds me of the day I left home to live and work overseas. As the train pulled out of the station, and I waved goodbye to my parents, we all knew that I would never again live permanently in my childhood home. I was setting out on a new chapter of my life, but it didn't feel like that. It felt as though I was severing all the connections that had ever held me safe, cutting myself off from the only life support I had ever known. It felt terrifying.

On that occasion I headed into unknown, though not particularly stormy waters. My Australian encounter with the force of the rip current pulled me into rather more traumatic seas where there was nothing I could do to help myself in spite of my best efforts to swim against the tide.

I would certainly not recommend doing battle with a rip current. The parting from our childhood home, however, is a different kind of weighing anchor and a necessary step along the path towards maturity. In the situation that surrounds us today, there is something of both these experiences. Political, social and geophysical upheavals have loosened our hold on the old anchorage. We have been shaken free of many of the old certainties. Some of this movement has been relatively steady as we have grown out of earlier assumptions and received wisdom and as we have collectively matured. In some ways however, it has felt more like being caught in a rip current. The very rapid changes that have overwhelmed us in recent years, and the tidal waves of political and social disruption have left very many people, in fact *most* people, in real fear of drowning.

It is no exaggeration to say that we have become unanchored.

Is the human boat now tossing helplessly on an angry sea?

Or is the human boat now being pitched into a new course, torn away from the old ropes that bound it to the harbour wall?

Is the emergent butterfly fluttering helplessly, exposed to all winds and weathers?

Or is the butterfly being released from its tether, to take its chance in a world that holds both delights and dangers?

It all depends on how you see the situation. The journey we have been making through these stages of transformation leads me to trust that our present experience of being unanchored can be a blessing not a curse – an invitation to grow, not a banishment into exile. Only the boat that dares to weigh anchor will sail anywhere. For the most part we would probably have chosen to stay in the old safe harbour (which was actually never as safe as we imagined), rather than risk the storms in which we now find ourselves, but life hasn't afforded us the luxury of choice. How the human story evolves from now on depends a great deal on our own attitude to the challenges we face.

SWORDS INTO PLOUGHSHARES

O n 21 March 2017 – the first day of spring – the breaking news in the UK was all about the death of Martin McGuinness, former commander of the paramilitary Irish Republican Army and a notorious hard fighter for the Republican cause in Ireland – a man who, inevitably, had made many bitter enemies, but who subsequently embraced, at great personal risk, the path of peace as deputy first minister in the devolved administration of Northern Ireland and became a major enabler of the Irish Peace Process. The journey of Martin McGuinness is a butterfly journey, not unlike that of Nelson Mandela before him. Mandela had also been a man of violence who, through the chrysalis time of his incarceration on Robben Island, emerged as the chief architect of a transformed, post-apartheid, South Africa.

The tributes to Martin McGuinness revealed, in a nutshell, the mysterious, but sacred, possibility of radical transformation from ruthless violence to courageous and visionary leadership in pursuit of peace and new ways forward. One tribute commented that it takes a big person to provide such big leadership.

Such greatness can manifest itself in great harm as well as great good. It reflects the reality of the 'shadow' in each human psyche. Psychologists tell us that the Shadow is a bit like an old cellar where we push all the stuff we don't want to have around in our conscious lives. Down in the cellar we can suppress it beyond the reach of memory. The strange thing is that we don't just suppress what we sense as harmful or even barbaric in our nature. We also suppress the very best in us, for fear of what our own inherent greatness might signify – almost, perhaps, for fear of 'challenging the gods'.

In the 'great leaders' such as McGuinness and Mandela and many others, we sometimes catch a glimpse of what is really down there in the human cellar – the very worst and the very best we can be. If we are searching for ways of becoming the best version of ourselves, we have much to learn from these colourful and powerful (in the best sense) figures of human history. The best, in them and in us, walks side by side with the worst. It lies in our choice, which of these potentialities will prevail.

The caterpillar shows us this dynamic in action. The immune system that so fiercely fights the emergence of the imaginal cells becomes the very means of nourishing their growth. What has been deeply divisive can become the glue of a new union, bringing forth a whole new harvest. What a vision for us in our present deep divisions and intractable conflicts. The stories of human beings whose lives have demonstrated this uneasy partnership between shadow and light can be beacons on our journey towards the more and more fully human being into which we are called to evolve.

Martin McGuinness died at the age of 66 from what was reported as 'a rare heart condition'. It is indeed a rare heart condition to be able to grow from the wielder of the sword to the maker of the ploughshare. He was joined, in Northern Irish politics, by his personal opponent, the flamboyant and vociferous unionist Ian Paisley. These two men clashed at every level, and very publicly. Their mutual antagonism was legendary. Yet each of them experienced a deep heart-change – so profound that they were able, ultimately, not only to work together to build the

Northern Ireland Peace Process, but also, even more remarkably, to become good friends.

The butterfly is the fruit of such a radical transformation from warmonger to peacemaker – from a threat to a promise. Spiritual traditions all issue a call to move in this direction. But miracles don't just happen inside the chrysalis. They happen in the human family, and in the most improbable and unlooked-for ways. And when we recognise them in action, we are invited to embrace the magic, rather than to settle into judgmental positions about the dark sides of our respective journeys. Where the light shines it will always cast a shadow. There is a real danger of defining ourselves and each other by our shadow, and failing to celebrate the light. If we do this, we might miss the dawn of the first day of spring.

WASPS AND
WILDFLOWERS

The migratory journeys of butterflies are motivated by two
overwhelming impulses that we also share:

The impulse to escape from mortal danger.

The impulse to seek out the food we need to live.

In our times we have begun to distinguish between 'refugees'
and 'economic migrants', and to be (perhaps half-heartedly)
welcoming of the former but resistant to the latter. Indeed,
the question of migration, so very imperfectly understood by
most of us, became the key driver of the vote of a small, but
determined margin of UK voters to leave the EU. On the question
of immigration very few of us pause to ask: 'What would I do
if my family were fleeing for our lives?'; 'What would I do if I
lacked the means to support my family, but knew I could find
it in another country?' Of course there are very real practical
challenges in accommodating a large influx of people into a
relatively small and hitherto stable country. Yet for a species
capable of developing space travel and artificial intelligence, is it
really impossible to find solutions to these problems?

The butterflies flee from the wasps – in particular those
specific wasps that have very bad intentions. These wasps inject
their eggs into the caterpillars and eat them up from the inside.
At worst they also inject a virus that modifies the caterpillar
genome. There is every reason to flee from this kind of attacker.

We may regard this bit of biological warfare as just one of

the many nasty strategies of the natural world, but if we dare to transpose it into our human situations what might we find? Not merely those who mean harm, and will attack us if they find us vulnerable, but those who would even 'eat us up from the inside' and alter the course of our future by modifying not our genome but our value systems. It isn't too hard to see how this threat has become an everyday reality in some regions of the world, especially in parts of Africa and the Middle East, where millions are fleeing not only from real and present danger, but also from the threat of having their children forcibly enlisted into brutal organisations and being subjected to such aggressive indoctrination as to undermine everything their parents would have desired for them. If we dare to look back into our own history, might we discover similar behaviour patterns of imperial force that we would much prefer not to have to acknowledge?

Is it just in the troubled regions of the world that we recognise this kind of threat? What 'wasps' are getting inside us, and eating us up from the inside? What subtle toxic movements are threatening to undermine our own value systems? What might de-rail the stability and emotional health of our own young? What personal issues are 'eating us up' and sapping our vital energy? These are crucial questions that we ignore at our peril. The butterflies know when they have to flee, and no barriers will prevent them from doing so. Do we really feel comfortable in setting up barriers against our fellow human beings who are also fleeing from mortal and horrible danger?

But the butterflies also follow the wildflower trail. They move from place to place in search of what they both desire and need in order to go on living and flourishing. The need, and the ability, to seek out food and life support is part of every creature's survival kit. We should also be mindful that we in the affluent west have historically always followed the wildflower trail ourselves, to many other parts of the world, in pursuit of a better life, and we are still doing so today. It ill behoves us to criticise those who now come to our lands in pursuit of the same dream. Just because we have everything we need for *our* survival in our own fields and pastures, or in the local supermarket, gives us absolutely no right to close our doors to others who are not so blessed. On the contrary, it places us under an obligation to be mindful of the needs of those who arrive on our shores, and to apply ourselves to solving the logistical problems that migration involves. A good manager says to his or her team: 'Don't bring me problems; bring me solutions.' We should be saying this to our politicians (as well as to ourselves), and insisting on results, on pain of dismissal and replacement (those great gifts of democracy).

The love affair between the flowers and the butterflies is mutual. Just as the butterflies love the nectar that the flowers offer them, so too the flowers welcome the butterflies, who pollinate them and make them fruitful. These 'economic migrants' bring with them more than they take away. As the UK continues its often acrimonious debate about migration, some of the more intelligent and insightful commentators keep reminding us that migrants very often contribute much more than they receive. In fact, like most nations, we are the product of historic migration, which over the centuries has 'pollinated' our society in ways we can never repay – except, just possibly, by starting to understand that as members of the human race we are all one and we are co-responsible for each other.

At the heart of the matter there is no 'them' and 'us'. The next stage of our spiritual evolution challenges us to take this fact on board, and to begin to live this new story and make it real.

MAKING THE
IDEAL REAL

'*If you have built castles in the air your work need not be lost.
That is where they should be. Now put the foundations under
them.*'

Henry David Thoreau

Putting the foundations under our castles in the air has been
the whole purpose of this book. But what do they look like in
practice?

Following a series of terrorist attacks within a short space of
time in the UK, and a catastrophic fire in a high rise tower block,
taking the lives of many men, women and children, and seriously
injuring many others, there was a remarkable outbreak of *love*.

This was no romantic loving, but the kind of loving that
risks itself for 'the other'. It revealed itself in some truly heroic
acts, in which emergency workers, as well as 'ordinary' unarmed,
unequipped people ran back into danger to help others, where
most were, very reasonably, running in the opposite direction.
Ancient wisdom tells us that the highest manifestation of love is
the willingness to put the life of another before our own. When
you witness this vision being lived out, and died for, on a summer
night in central Manchester or London, you begin to believe in the
possibility of a transformed humanity taking shape in the here and
now. A clue that this is happening is when the talk is predominantly
and explicitly of love, rather than of reproach or revenge.

There were also many less dramatic, but equally significant acts of human goodness. There always are, wherever disaster strikes. Demonstrations of kindness like those who offer emergency accommodation, and taxi drivers who provide free transportation to those who are stranded. Like the man who came back the morning after a Saturday night attack in London, asking permission to go through the police cordons, because he wanted to check on the proprietor of the restaurant that he had been forced to evacuate in the emergency – and to pay his bill.

These are small stones to add to the foundations of the building of a new humanity, you might think, but there are over seven billion human beings on the planet, engaged in this great work, and that amounts to a very large pile of foundation stones. These small acts of heroic humanity have been reflected in similar situations throughout the world, flying in the face of fear, and amplifying the assurance that, truly, the light shines in the darkness and the darkness does not have the power to extinguish it.

A good way forward might be to become more consciously aware of the challenge to put foundations under our castle, and to reflect, intentionally, on our daily lives in the light of this aspiration, making adjustments where we notice shortfalls, and nourishing the positive, in ourselves and others.

There will be many voices telling us that building castles in the air is a futile enterprise, and, even more disturbingly, they may ask us whether this whole adventure is just a circular journey. At the end of the day the butterfly just lays another egg, and the whole story goes round once again. Is there really any progression, at least for the human family? It's a matter of faith of course. It's a story that may or not be true, but if we live that story – the story of potential transformation, then in very real ways that story becomes more and more true with every passing generation, just as the butterfly's impossible journey becomes not only possible, but inevitable, if it is received and welcomed with gratitude and humility from those who have gone before us, lived authentically in our own lives, times and places, and then passed on to those who follow after us, as they in their turn carry the vision a little bit closer towards its fulfilment.

When we reflect on the bigger story that enfolds us, we may begin to see that this isn't a circular journey, simply bringing us back to where we began, only to start another iteration. Rather it is a spiral journey. The spiral of our own lives, and the life of our nation, our generation, and even of the whole human family, may spiral upwards, bringing us a little closer to the Omega, or downwards, drawing us further away from that fulfilment. The direction depends on our choices. Every choice we make will either move the spiral upwards or downwards a little. Neutral isn't an option. If we believe the spiral story, and throw our energy into it, it will become the real story, whatever the cynics may tell us.

It isn't a stretch to claim that we are building a kin-dom with our lives. The blueprint is there for our castle in the air. The architect's plans are approved. Our task is to place the foundation stones beneath the dream as Thoreau invites us.

How do we do it? Well, the task of building this foundation proceeds one human life, one personal choice, at a time and these words from Ken Wilbur offer a good recipe:

Be the most ethical, the most responsible, the most authentic you can be with every breath you take, because you are cutting a path into tomorrow that others will follow.

OMEGA

Promises, promises....

We began our journey with the story of an unlikely promise made by a dying woman, and fulfilled in her remarkable appearance at her own funeral. It was the promise of a winged and transformed life hovering over human pain and loss, and settling on it with the gentlest of touches, bringing hope and consolation.

It is unlikely that within the limitations of our human condition we will ever be able to experience the fullness of the Omega point on this side of the great mystery. Omega will probably remain always a step beyond our mortal horizon but the horizon itself is an invitation to keep on searching, and to keep on evolving.

It would be wonderful to end this journey with a vision of the Omega, but for that we are still stuck this side of the horizon, so any such vision would be highly speculative.

No beatific vision therefore, not at this stage in our evolution, but instead, another promise – an Omega promise in response to the Alpha promise.

Ali's Alpha promise is that there is much more than we can possibly imagine. It defies all our definitions of what is reasonable or possible. But it is discovered out of, and through, the frightening meltdown of dissolution and death – whether this is the death of our bodies or the death of our hopes, dreams and expectations.

Our response is our Omega promise, to commit ourselves to

live our lives and make our choices in ways that contribute to the spiritual evolution of humankind, and to create the foundation stones that will underpin the vision

The vision is to play our part as co-creators of a new kin-dom, which ancient scripture assures us is already present within us. A kin-dom needs a constitution, so one possible approach to embracing this Omega-promise and giving it substance is the new 'constitution' that follows.

I invite you, as a closing exercise, to reflect on this Constitution and maybe write your own – either individually or as a group.

The purpose of this exercise is not just to formulate a wish-list for our Omega-Becoming, but to make a real and practical commitment to bringing us closer to the best Humanity we can become.

It is a statement of our desire and intent to live purposefully towards the great call of transformation.

A NEW CONSTITUTION FOR A NEW CONSCIOUSNESS

Though we are many – there are currently some 7.5 billion human beings on the planet – we are one. We all emerge from the same source in the heart of a mystery we might call love, and we all strive towards the same destiny in the heart of that mystery.

We are one with each other, and we are one with all life on this living planet.

In all our decisions we honour, before all else, our responsibility for the health and wellbeing of our planet and all the creatures who share it with us. We commit ourselves to do everything in our power to protect our planet, and to avoid, resist and oppose all that might jeopardise it.

We acknowledge that the energy of transformation derives from a source infinitely greater than our own, but that we are also challenged to become co-creators of the future we desire.

We recognise that the future we create tomorrow depends on the moment-by-moment choices we make today. Some of these choices seem tiny and some seem huge. Every one of them matters, and will either draw us a little bit closer to the best we can be, or pull us a little bit further away from the future we desire.

We undertake to make all our choices responsibly, mindfully, and for the greater good of all creation.

We commit ourselves to strive for equality, which means that we will not privilege ourselves, our own tribe, generation, social class, country or religious tradition at the expense of others. We recognise that what is life-giving for all of us is also life-giving for each of us, and that what harms any of us harms all of us.

We understand that transformation can only be experienced through the traumatic meltdown of the chrysalis. We know that this is a dark and potentially frightening place, where we will feel helpless, voiceless and blind. We will trust this process and support each other whenever we have to pass through chrysalis times in our lives and in the life of the world.

We rejoice that we already carry our own best future within us, just as the butterfly is already present within the caterpillar. We rejoice that even though circumstances may appear to destroy us, nothing can ever destroy the dream we hold in our hearts. We commit ourselves to trust the dream, to nourish the dream in each other and to live towards its fulfilling.

We desire to learn from the butterflies the art of symbiotic relationships, and we will strive to live in such a way that we do not take without also giving, that we never take what we desire by harming or invading another living being, including the earth herself, and that every interaction we have with any other living being is a source of enrichment for all involved

Like the butterflies, we respect every other living being that shares our space. We commit ourselves never to demonise those with different beliefs, opinions or lifestyles, but to engage in compassionate listening, so that we may gradually grow into deeper understanding of 'the other' without compromising our own integrity.

Like the butterflies we commit ourselves to care for our

young and for the generations who follow after us, guiding them towards what nourishes them, safeguarding them from all that would harm them, passing on to them the wisdom of the way, gleaned from our own reflected experience and, when the time is right, making way for them, passing on to them the baton of life.

We recognise that we are on a journey. The journey is taking us from Alpha to Omega – from where we are now, to the best we can be. We know that we can't yet see, or even imagine, what that Omega will mean, but we do have glimpses of it, for example in the greatest human beings and, especially for Christians, in Jesus of Nazareth. We commit ourselves to live true in our own way, using our own particular gifts, to the vision we have glimpsed.

We know that on this journey we will encounter both wasps and wildflowers – deadly threats and great blessings. We commit ourselves to support each other through the hazards, and to share the blessings. We further commit ourselves to avoid ever becoming a hazard to others, but rather, as far as we are able, to live as a blessing.

We recognise that this journey is a Journey of Becoming, an evolutionary work-in-progress. We commit ourselves to *become the change we long for*, just as the imaginal cell gradually becomes its own unique part of the butterfly. To do this we each undertake to strive to become the best human being we can be, and to come together in peaceful and whole-hearted collaboration to become the best humanity we can collectively be.

We recognise that we cannot do this alone, but only in the sustaining and enabling power of the holy mystery that birthed us, and in active co-operation with each other both in our own community and generation, and across the global community and generations still unborn.

A NEW CONSTITUTION

We rejoice that, though we are still immature caterpillars fighting each other and the rest of the forest for survival, unheeding of the harm we cause, nevertheless we hold the future within us, and from the first moment of our hatching, we were born to fly.

ACKNOWLEDGEMENTS

A book is always the product of many minds and of the interconnection of many hearts.

I would like especially to thank David Moloney, Helen Porter and Judy Linard of Darton, Longman and Todd for your personal encouragement and enthusiasm, careful editing and creative design.

Thank you to Jane Besly and Annette White, for so kindly reading and responding to the early draft, also Marianne and Robin Anker-Petersen, Beth Roberton, Kath Saltwell, Mary Saucier, Benedicte Scholefield, Trish and Richard Young, and all who have made the 'butterfly journey' and helped me navigate today's political minefield.

I am greatly in debt to the unique thought and wisdom of Pierre Teilhard de Chardin on the process of human evolution and transformation and to Louis M. Savary who has made these insights so accessible and relevant for our own times, especially in his books *The Divine Milieu Explained* and *The New Spiritual Exercises*.

I also gratefully acknowledge the work of Yuval Noah Harari on human development, and the power of story, presented so compellingly in his books *Sapiens* and *Homo Deus*.

Not infrequently, in these troubled times, I have felt close to slipping the wrong side of zero in my own faith in the future. It has been the love and support of my family, Kirstin, Paul, Alexa and Isabella, and my circle of soul-friends from Keele and from the Stoke Quaker Meeting, who never fail to draw me back to the stlll centre at the heart of every storm.